YOUR SMALL BUSINESS ADVENTURE

YOUR SMALL BUSINESS ADVENTURE

FINDING YOUR NICHE AND GROWING A SUCCESSFUL BUSINESS

JAMES W. HALLORAN

an imprint of the American Library Association

HURON STREET PRESS

CHICAGO · 2014

In 1987 **James W. Halloran** wrote the best-selling book, *The Entrepreneur's Guide to Starting a Successful Business,* which became a Book-of-the-Month selection and was one of the first books to introduce the concept of "entrepreneurship" into our everyday vocabulary. Twenty-five years and eight books later, Halloran is still writing and encouraging entrepreneurs throughout the United States and the world. His books have been translated into foreign languages and he has taught and lectured at colleges and universities throughout the United States. Halloran resides with his wife Diane in Madison, Georgia, where he continues to write, consult, and own a small business. To contact Jim, view his website at www.jwhalloran.com.

Printed in the United States of America
18 17 16 15 14   5 4 3 2 1

Extensive effort has gone into ensuring the reliability of the information in this book; however, the publisher makes no warranty, express or implied, with respect to the material contained herein.

ISBN: 978–1-937589-44-8 (paper)

Library of Congress Cataloging-in-Publication Data
Halloran, James W.
   Your small business adventure : finding your niche and growing a successful business / James W. Halloran.
      pages   cm
   Includes bibliographical references and index.
   ISBN 978-1-937589-44-8 (alk. paper)
   1. New business enterprises. 2. Small business—Management. I. Title.
HD62.5.H3534 2014
658.1'1—dc23

                                                                    2013043136

Book design by Kimberly Thornton in Gotham and Chapparal Pro.
Image © N. Réka/Shutterstock, Inc.

♾ This paper meets the requirements of ANSI/NISO Z39.48–1992 (Permanence of Paper).

The mass of men lead lives of quiet desperation.
What is called desperation is confirmed resignation.

—Henry David Thoreau

This book is dedicated to all those who have chosen not to live in resignation by taking the risk of starting a business. These entrepreneurs and, in particular, the mom and pop business owners, are the backbone of our economy as they quietly create jobs, discover better ways to do things, and contribute to the betterment of our society through the taxes they pay and the services they perform.

A great appreciation to my wife Diane for her patience, input, and proofreading skills and the staff at ALA Editions for their help in putting this book together.

CONTENTS

INTRODUCTION

"FOR OVER 4 YEARS I HAVE BEEN RIDING THIS SAME ELEVATOR, AT THE SAME time, every morning and evening, 4½ years, and what I have accomplished—it's depressing. Standing here with the same people, some who have been doing this for 10, 20 years and even more, going to the same place, stuck in the same routine."

These were the thoughts going through Chuck's mind as he ascended to his assigned place as the call center director for a large insurance company. Chuck had arrived in his new job about the same time the economy was collapsing. The promises of promotions and moving up the corporate ladder had disappeared. Raises and bonuses were minimal, morale of fellow employees was low—a frustrating time for sure. Everyone kept telling him he should be happy just to have a job but that could only carry him for so long. Chuck wanted growth, challenge, and excitement but where could he find it? Now he, like so many, was feeling stagnant and the longer it went on the harder it was to cover up his disappointment. He wondered if there was opportunity outside the corporate world—maybe as a business owner.

But was now the time to take such a risk? Maybe he could start a part-time business which could grow. Where should he start the search to answer this question?

That is what this book is going to probe. Is there opportunity? Where should *you* look? What can you learn from those who preceded you in such an undertaking? The process starts with a close look at you. Your aptitude, attitude, and perseverance to achieve will be the guide in the search. If you place yourself in the right environment and surround yourself with enough tangible and intangible assets, you can achieve success beyond what many prognosticators may predict.

Part I of the book, "Where Do You Belong?" starts with an in-depth personal career analysis test to assist in finding the most compatible arena for your pursuits. This will be followed by an examination of your VANE (values, attitudes, needs, and expectations) to more clearly define the appropriate path for you to follow and build a personal entrepreneur profile. You will be asked to match your ideas to these important factors and also compare your personal characteristics to those who have found success as entrepreneurs. At the conclusion of this study of you, various business avenues will be cited along with a description of what should be expected in the various endeavors. This will include a look at part-time businesses and the attractiveness of starting a business on the side and allowing it to grow while you stay employed.

Part II, "The Common Pitfalls—What Not to Do," will cite the common and often repeated mistakes of aspiring entrepreneurs. You will visit entrepreneurs with problems and see how to face them because you will certainly encounter many of these difficulties. These situations will test the validity of your entrepreneurial profile.

Part III, "The Yellow Brick Road," the last section, will lead you to successful strategies to follow in starting and managing a business. It too will be supported by stories of entrepreneurs, but in this instance we see how successful strategies put them ahead of the game. Building on the strengths of your compatibility will allow you to develop such strategies.

The final outcome will be a path for you to follow in determining where you fit into the world of entrepreneurship. Which type of entrepreneurial career is best for you? How can you avoid the most common mistakes and what strategies can you develop that will lead to success?

Whether you are like Chuck and feel stuck in a hamster's revolving cage wheel, or among the millions of dispirited underemployed or unemployed, this book will serve you well as you look to your future.

PART I

Where do you belong?

The first five chapters are designed to make you think about the decisions you made in the past and how they can lead you to the correct decisions for your future. There is a self-analysis questionnaire to stimulate the thought process along with a series of analytical questions. You will then take the time to give thoughtful consideration to the values that matter most to you and whether your attitude can pass the entrepreneurial challenges. What environment should you seek? What type of selling situation are you most comfortable with? Finally, there is a glimpse into various types of business arenas and what they really are as opposed to what you might think or hope they are.

Let's get started.

Entrepreneur

He casts away his assurance of forty-hour weeks,
leaves the safe cover of tenure and security,
and charges across the perilous fields of change
and opportunity. If he succeeds, his profits will
come not from what he takes from his fellow
citizens, but from the value they freely place
on the gift of his imagination.
—*George Gilder*

Who Are You?

THIS SEEMS TO BE A RECURRING QUESTION FOR MANY OF US. ONE THING FOR sure, we do not wish to be underemployed, unemployed, or in any position that does not challenge us to the fullest. Being challenged is exciting and it stimulates us into doing things we did not think possible. It also gives us purpose and provides a feeling of self-achievement when we are successful. In other words, challenge is good for us, so let's start there. *You belong in an environment and occupation that challenge you.*

The starting place to find where we should be going is by looking at where we have been. In what situations have we felt that excitement? Was it in a past job, a hobby, a sport, a particular event?

Over twenty years ago Edgar H. Schein of the Massachusetts Institute of Technology created a test, Career Anchors, that has been used primarily in the corporate world to place employees. Its success is derived from the theory that by looking at past decisions and why they were made, we can get a clearer understanding of what motivates us in our work. With a few tweaks we can use the basis of this test to determine your entrepreneurial base and what type of business environment fits your personal psychological makeup. Our goal is to determine which of the entrepreneurial base categories fit you and how that entrepreneurial base can direct you to the type of entrepreneurial opportunities in which you will prosper personally and financially. Is it perfect? No, but as a counselor and consultant I have used it with amazing success for over twenty years.

Entrepreneurial Base Test: A Two-Step Process

STEP ONE: THIRTY-QUESTION PERSONAL EXAMINATION

Take twenty minutes to answer the following 30 questions. Score your answers by ranking how you feel about each statement from 1 to 5. Go with your first reaction in determining how true the description fits you.

(1) Not at All   (2) Occasionally True   (3) Often True   (4) Mostly True
(5) Fits You Perfectly

_____ 1. Being able to do a job well is more important than pay or timeliness.

_____ 2. I will feel successful only if I can maintain a healthy balance of work with family.

_____ 3. A business is only successful if it contributes to its community.

_____ 4. I stay away from confrontation with my boss when our ideas clash.

_____ 5. I would not seek a job that does not offer a complete benefit package.

_____ 6. In meetings I often volunteer new ideas and ways for doing things.

_____ 7. If you can't do a job right, don't do it at all.

_____ 8. Mixing leisure and work is essential for success.

_____ 9. I enjoy performing volunteer work.

_____ 10. I dreamed of owning a business even before graduating from school.

_____ 11. Being paid twice a month versus monthly is important as it makes budgeting much easier.

_____ 12. I prefer not to get involved with brainstorming sessions at work.

_____ 13. Praise for doing my job well makes my day.

_____ 14. I enjoy having weekends to spend with family and friends.

_____ 15. "It takes a village" is an overstated declaration.

_____ 16. I would prefer to work alone as opposed to a group project.

_____ 17. I don't know what I would do if I got laid off from my job.

_____ 18. When I see a stream I want to know its origin.

_____ 19. When I am working on a project I get very upset when interrupted.

_____ 20. I enjoy attending large parties.

_____ 21. The U.S.A. needs to worry more about its economy and less about helping foreign nations.

_____ 22. If my team is losing I will often leave a sporting event early to beat the traffic.

_____ 23. I become very anxious when confronted with change in my job environment.

_____ 24. As a child I used to enjoy performing magic tricks.

_____ 25. I would prefer to work on my hobby than attend a cocktail party.

_____ 26. I enjoy planning social events.

_____ 27. Health care is a right which all should receive equally.

_____ 28. I do not ask for directions when I am uncertain as to how to find a location.

_____ 29. Getting recognition for length of service is an important acknowledgment.

_____ 30. I often become very restless and fail to pay attention during meetings at work.

Record your scores for each question below. Review any questions that you scored a 5 and add three points to the three that you feel most strongly about.

EXP	LS	SER	CI	STB	IC
1. 1	2. 2	3. 4	4. 1	5. 1	6. 2
7. 4	8. 4	9. 2	10. 5	11. 4	12. 1
13. 2	14. 4	15. 1	16. 1	17. 1	18. 2
19. 3	20. 2	21. 5 +3	22. 3	23. 2	24. 1
25. 5 +3	26. 4	27. 5 +3	28. 1	29. 3	30. 3

TOTALS:

18   16   23   11   11   10

Divide each column total by 6 to get the average score for that column:

3   2   4   2   2   2

List the headings from the top with the average score for each, highest total to lowest, and then read below for a description of each entrepreneurial base.

Highest scoring category: _Ser_   **Avg. score:** _4_

Exp   _3_

_LS_   _2_

_CI_   _2_

_S+B_   _2_

Lowest scoring category: _IC_   **Avg. score:** _2_

Entrepreneurial Base Scoring

Review the questionnaire scores with the following descriptions of entrepreneurial bases.

EXP: Expertise. Those who score high in this column enjoy doing precise work and doing it well. Receiving recognition for a job well done is more important than pay or promotions. These individuals desire opportunities that allow them to develop expertise in their field. When they are working outside of their field of expertise they feel uncomfortable. Their identity is built around the content of their work more than titles or awards. They commit to a life of specialization and challenge in their particular field.

LS: Lifestyle. Individuals with a high lifestyle base score desire to build their careers around a desired lifestyle. They set personal priorities very high. A job that infringes upon these priorities is not acceptable. Often they are not team or corporate players. Lifestyle individuals are determined to integrate personal and family interests with career. They choose jobs with organizations that express a strong attitude for family values. They want flexibility in their work assignments whether it involves where they are located, how much travel is required, or working hours.

SER: Service to Others. This base is for those with a strong desire to reach out to others and want a career that fulfills this need. They have certain values that they wish to embody in their work and these values drive their decisions and ambitions. Often they work in public, not-for-profit service arenas or organizations with a strong commitment to creating products or services that help society. Money is not the prime motivator and is secondary to societal contribution.

CI: Challenge/Independence. A high CI base score is for those who are willing to take on challenges above and beyond what is expected. They are extremely confident and competitive individuals who feel they can conquer almost any challenge. They are never satisfied with the status quo, always looking to the next goal. They desire to be in control of their own destiny, captain of their own ship. CI individuals do not like supervision. They define life in competitive terms. These individuals are not tied into expertise as they are willing to move their efforts into multiple areas. Multitasking fits them well. They seek work that offers constant challenge in competitive environments, such as sales.

STB: Stability. People who have a deep yearning for stability and are apprehensive regarding change make up this classification. Organization life is fine for them provided they are treated fairly. They wish to be recognized for loyalty and commitment to the organization. In exchange for this they work hard and share the belief that what is good for the organization is good for them. If not treated fairly they will react emotionally and lose their interest and will look elsewhere if their needs are not met. "Golden handcuffs" are fine with them provided they believe in the work they are doing. Benefits programs are as important as pay. Promotions based on seniority are acceptable and often preferable. Tenure positions are greatly desired.

IC: Individual Creativity. This base refers to those who like to create, offer new ideas, and explore new ways of doing a task. They possess a creative urge and are often considered dreamers. They are normally not content with traditional organizations with numerous levels of hierarchy. They do not want a boss who will steal their ideas without giving them credit. They desire recognition and rewards for their ideas. IC individuals are good at leading brainstorming sessions. Often they will not stay long with a project as they are anxious to move on to the next new thing.

STEP TWO: INTERVIEW ASSESSMENT

Before we label you with an entrepreneurial base monitor there is another important step to undertake. As mentioned, we start with an examination of your past decisions. The next step is an interview session with a partner that examines the reasons for past decisions and the satisfaction derived from those decisions. If you are just now starting a career and there are questions that do not apply directly to you, think back to jobs you worked during your education and how you and fellow workers thought about them as possible stepping-stones. Take the time to discuss in depth the following twelve questions and make notes when appropriate. Our goal here is to make sure the initial assessment from the previous questions is valid. After completing the interview and reflecting back on the questionnaire scoring, you should be able to determine your entrepreneurial base. These questions will also allow you to more distinctly identify your base in the event the test score results are closely huddled together.

1. What areas of your education brought you the greatest feeling of excitement? (Note: This does not necessarily equate with greatest success.) Why did you choose to study these areas? Would you choose the same areas now?

2. What was your goal in selecting your first job after graduation? Did this job match your objective? Why or why not?

3. What was the first change you encountered in your career? Good or bad? How did it make you feel? Did it challenge you?

4. Trace other changes in your career path. Which ones brought satisfaction and challenge, which ones did not? Why? Why not?

5. When was the first time the thought of owning a business first crossed your mind? What was that idea? Is it still foremost?

6. Are you a daydreamer? Are your daydreams realistic?

7. What particular events and transitions have you enjoyed in your career? Why? What ones have proven to be a disappointment?

8. Have you ever said no to a job change or challenge? If so, what was it that made it unacceptable?

9. Describe your career to this point in terms of personal satisfaction.

10. Looking down the road ten years, what do you see? Where will you live? What will you do? What are your family goals?

11. Describe the best boss you have worked for. Why was he or she the best? Describe the worst boss. What created that feeling?

12. What makes you feel anxious? How do you deal with anxiety?

Discuss each answer in terms of how it fits your initial assessment from the entrepreneurial base questionnaire. Keep in mind that the objective is to determine what has given you satisfaction, or dissatisfaction, in the past in order to ensure that you will consider entering a new endeavor that will provide the necessary incentive to perform to your fullest potential.

Can you share entrepreneurial base classifications? Yes, but usually one will stand out. Can your entrepreneurial base change? Yes, depending on your stage in life. For example, a person with a challenge/independence base at a young age may test out as a lifestyle entrepreneur later on in their life.

Once you are satisfied with your assigned entrepreneurial description, we will start to explore in the following chapters the types of entrepreneurial environment that you may wish to consider.

Applying What You Have Learned about Yourself

Don't be disappointed, but we are not going to tell you the perfect business for you to explore based on the above exercises. What we will do is advise you as to what arena or environment best suits your ambitions based on your past decisions. Once determined, we will examine your choices even further in the following chapters.

Expertise entrepreneurs are suited for work that allows them to develop a particular skill or intellectual trait. This might range from a car mechanic to a computer geek. The idea is to give you the freedom to develop your objective with a minimum amount of interference. Expertise entrepreneurs will not be happy nor as productive if they are wearing multiple hats and performing multitask jobs. If your highest score was expertise and it was validated after your interview, look around for opportunities that provide you with this environment. Examples of possibilities include: craft work, woodworking, mechanic, software development, medical technician in a specific field, actuarial assignments, accounting/bookkeeping, and engineering fields.

Lifestyle entrepreneurs are becoming more common. Not long ago when an employee was asked to move he or she would respond with "where to?" Now it is "I will need to consider it, I have personal obligations where I am." The combination of dual career families, technology, and a generation more willing to ask " why" has changed the playing field. Employees are seeking more control of their lives, and when demands become excessive they are willing to move onto something else just like you are considering in becoming self-employed. If you rated high on lifestyle make sure that your choice of pursuit does not conflict with your lifestyle priorities. In the next chapter we will have you look closely at what you hold dearly and advise you not to abandon them. Completing the lifestyle profile in chapter 2 should enable you to draw a line on how much you are willing to sacrifice to receive your independence.

Service to others means exactly that. You will not be satisfied in work that does not make a contribution to the betterment of society or to your community in which you live. This does not mean you are not an entrepreneur— many not-for-profit organizations are founded by entrepreneurs. They use their entrepreneurial drive to raise funds in the ever increasingly competitive marketplace of not-for-profit organizations. If this is you, great—start thinking about the type of not-for-profit organization that you would like to lead.

Challenge and independence classification sounds like the ideal candidate for an entrepreneurial pursuit. Yes and no. This anchor possesses the very important competitive instincts of the entrepreneur in combination with the self-confidence to do it alone. Good so far but . . . be careful. This base does not like discipline and can get into trouble without it. If this is you go for it, but consider taking along a colleague to keep you in line and follow up on the routine details that go with starting a business. Owning a business requires more than being risk-bearing, creative, and imaginative. Reports must be filed, financial statements must be kept, policies determined, and so on, or the business will lose its focus. A challenge/independence entrepreneur should look at competitive industries in which sales and outmaneuvering your opponent will win out.

Stability entrepreneurs have a tough time making the transition to self-employment but should not rule out the possibility if it is truly a desire.

There can be some safe havens out there such as buying into a very established franchise system or buying a very successful, established business. These opportunities will most likely cost more to enter but they will offer more security in exchange for the more expensive upfront cost. The seller in this case is getting paid for the years invested in building a successful business. If possible you should buy a successful business from a company or owner who will help you with the transition.

Individual creativity individuals are equipped with very strong entrepreneurial traits to consider self-employment. Success will come from those who think of a better way to do things. Whether that means better products, customer service, preferable location, or more exciting marketing campaigns—it gets down to doing it better than your competition. Your business does not have to be the best in the world, only the best in your marketplace. You do not have to reinvent the wheel for success. You have to outthink the competition and this requires creativity. Every time the opponent makes a move, you need to make a countermove. The creative juices should never take a day off. This individual will serve any business well but in particular look at businesses that are in public view—retailing, advertising, public relations, and entertainment businesses all fit this description.

Chapter Story

CHOOSING AN INCOMPATIBLE BUSINESS

Woody had spent his entire 22-year career as an airline pilot for a major commercial airline. Labor and management problems threatened to close the airline—a very anxious time for Woody. He was too old to be considered a young hotshot who could easily catch on with another airline and too young to consider retirement. He knew he must prepare for a new career if the company collapsed, which it did.

Woody developed a friendship with Bob, the owner of a local yogurt store chain. "Great business with great profit potential, Woody, as long as you work hard and keep an eye on things." It sounded perfect to Woody. He spent a Saturday working with Bob at one of his stores and excitedly reported to his wife, Ann, that he had found what he wanted to do. Ann worried about Woody's lack of business experience, but Woody was insistent that this was right for him. Shortly after the airline's demise Woody signed a three-year lease for a 1,200-square-foot store on the outside of a new mall. He borrowed $75,000, using his house as collateral, and with Bob's help ordered all equipment and supplies needed to open the store.

Sixty days later, Woody was the unhappiest he had ever been. He absolutely hated the yogurt business. Working seven days a week, supervising a teenage workforce, and being confined to the 1,200-square-foot store was as far from what he was used to as he could get. Business had started slowly, further depressing him. He was making poor business decisions, was irritable at home, and couldn't sleep thinking of his large sinking investment. He looked to the sky with every passing airplane. Why, he thought, did he ever think he should be a retailer? He belonged in aviation, not in a shopping center.

Soon after, Woody took the advice of Ann and his friends and put the store up for sale. His goal was to get out. Priced at the $75,000 originally invested, he found a buyer within a couple of months. The terms were not great, $10,000 down and the rest over five years. The buyer was a divorced woman in need of a career. Six months into the agreement she backed out. Business was weak and she was marrying and moving out of state. "It's all yours, Woody. You will have to take it back. By the way I am a couple of months behind on the rent." Now Woody was in worse shape. The landlord threatened to claim the property if the rent was not paid, so Woody had to write a check for almost half the down payment he had received from the buyer—he was back in the yogurt business. What made it worse was that he had gotten back into aviation as the manager of an avionics supply business and he was totally enjoying this new experience helping private pilots. He feared he would have to leave this new opportunity to protect his investment in the yogurt business, which he now hated with a passion. In desperation he called Bob Sinclair and offered him the business for whatever he felt was fair. Luckily Bob gave a reasonable settlement. Although much of the investment was lost, Woody was finally out from under his predicament and now able to work in the environment best suited for him.

It is obvious that Woody's background was never compatible with the yogurt or any retail-oriented business. Spending one Saturday working in such a store does not provide enough research to make such an important decision. Woody acted impulsively and emotionally instead of taking the time to properly analyze himself and opportunities. He is an expertise entrepreneur. He had spent twenty-two years gaining expertise in flying and understanding the aviation industry. He developed a skill set of which he was proud. Now he can use that skill set in working with pilots surrounded by airplanes and someday maybe own an avionics supply business. A close examination of his past would have kept him from rushing into a business environment better suited for a creativity or challenge entrepreneur.

Closing Tip

Continue to reexamine your entrepreneurial base description by asking those who know you and your past career stages well if they agree with your assessment.

2

Values, Attitudes, Needs, and Expectations

NTREPRENEURSHIP IS ABOUT MUCH MORE THAN MAKING MONEY. AT ITS CORE is the personal satisfaction that owning a business brings to the risk taker. Entrepreneurs work for their own goals, not the goals of others. They are able to set their own priorities, and most important, they enjoy their work. This is only possible if you match your values, attitude, needs, and expectations (VANE) to your endeavor. Step two of our process is to make sure that your entrepreneur anchor is in sync with your VANE before deciding on a specific opportunity.

Values. What beliefs and convictions do you hold most dear? What are the essential tangibles and intangibles that add to your life—the things you cannot do without? Are they present in the opportunity you seek? Study the following list of important life values and rank them in regard to your happiness.

Achievement—sense of fulfillment
Adventure—excitement, exploration, risk

Authenticity—genuine

Enjoyment—in regards to work

Expertness—being good at something important

Family—ample time with family, contented living situation

Friendship—association with others

Independence—making your own choices

Intellect—mind utilization

Leadership—using influence and authority

Location—where you live

Loyalty—to give and receive

Meaningful work—relevancy and purpose

Money—how much is enough to provide your desired needs

Physical health—vitality

Prestige—recognition for your efforts, how you are seen by others

Security—stability

Self-growth—personal development

Service—contribution to others

Spirituality—religious beliefs

Of course all these values are important, but are there some that rank higher or may not apply to your personal scale. Keep them in mind as you proceed through this chapter while you build a personal profile.

Attitude. How do you view life and the environment that surrounds you? Steven Covey in his well-known book, *The 7 Habits of Highly Effective People,* illustrates how attitude forms a habitual way of viewing things. Pessimists have developed the habit of viewing their surroundings in a negative manner, optimists of course in a positive manner. As we know, habits are difficult to change; it takes effort and practice. If you do not feel optimistic and confident regarding your choice of venture you will fail. It is imperative that you have a positive attitude about your undertaking. If not, put it on hold.

Needs. Needs are the tangible and intangible things that you feel you must have to maintain or acquire an acceptable lifestyle. It is important to truthfully recognize these needs as they will serve as the motivators for you to go forward. It will also be important for you to understand the needs of your customers in order to motivate them to purchase your product or service. Needs include how you feel about yourself and how others see you.

Expectations. In determining your expectations of what to receive from your initial venture, state them as minimum goals you hope to achieve. As your business opportunity grows, so can your expectations. We sometimes suffer from "greener pasture" syndrome. Look closely before you leap.

Review some past incidents of your career and personal life and declare how they made you feel. Circle the ones that are particularly outstanding, whether positive or negative. This will help identify the actions that have had the most impact in achieving personal satisfaction or dissatisfaction. The following chart is an example.

INCIDENT VALUE CORRELATION	ATTITUDE	NEED	EXPECTATION
Employee of the month	positive	job security	met
Family trip	family positive	belonging	met
No promotion	loss of prestige	loss of status	not met
Quit smoking	health/achievement	physiological	met
Scuba diving adventure	positive	self-actualization	met
Visit disabled elder	authenticity	positive self esteem	met

Keep your VANE in mind as you review and fill out the following personal goal guide.

Your Personal Goals

In considering entrepreneurship you should be declaring your right to do what you want to do. Since this is your personal declaration of independence, make sure the goals you set will accomplish your declaration. However, at the same time you must be realistic in regard to the assets and abilities that you are able to bring to the table.

Income. Income goals must be set in consideration of not only a great idea but also in regard to the size of investment and degree of risk. There is a direct correlation between the amount of money and time invested and the amount of profit a business generates in its beginning stages. Over time experience, perseverance, and creativity will play a bigger role, but initially it takes money to make money. Rare is the business that can be started with a $10,000 investment and return an immediate profit of $100,000. The initial stages usually require financial sacrifices not only in regard to investing personal income but also as to income generated. This does not mean you should be thinking that you will lose money in your first year, but recognize that meaningful profits will most likely have to be reinvested in order for the business to grow. Set income goals in phases: year one, two, and three. Your year-one goal should be the minimum amount of money you will need to meet your personal obligations. Hopefully it will be more than that, but at the very least you are making sure that you can keep your head above water while the business matures. This goal may eliminate an idea or change its direction because you should not proceed without some feeling of certainty that this minimal goal will be attained. It may also lead you to investigate part-time business opportunities that can grow into full-time occupations while you continue your present employment. (See chapter 5.)

Personal satisfaction. As mentioned, it is not about the money as much as receiving personal satisfaction from what you accomplish. Whether that is contributing to one's family, community, or country, personal satisfaction factors motivate us to reach our highest potential of achievement. It is important to declare the following.

The type of work which brings satisfaction. For some it may be working outdoors, while others enjoy working with numbers or sales. Remember that you are declaring what you want out of life. Small businesses come in all forms, shapes, and sizes. Some will require you to work directly with and through many people, others will allow you to work alone. You choose what fits you.

Lifestyle: how much involvement is required. Not all businesses require working 60 or 70 hours of work per week. Many lifestyle entrepreneurs enter self-employment to work less and enjoy leisure time more. Some will look for businesses that can be managed from a distance as absentee managers. How do you feel about working evenings, weekends, travel—this is the time to declare your priorities in accordance with your VANE. Of course, less involvement may also translate into less personal income.

Community involvement. There are businesses that require you to be active in community or industry projects or organizations in order to network with potential clients. Others do not have such demands. Which do you prefer?

Capabilities. The abilities you have developed play an important role in your career decision-making process. Take an inventory of your strengths and weaknesses. Review your entrepreneur base interview questionnaire. Build on and utilize your strengths and recognize where you need help in terms of both mental and physical attributes or weaknesses. Also inventory your financial capabilities. Determine not only what monies are available but also how much you are willing to risk. Are there others you need to take into consideration? How much risk you are willing to take is an indication of confidence, but you cannot be reckless or irresponsible. See table 2.2, "Determining Personal Capital Available."

Use the following table as a guideline for building a personal profile. Analyze each factor closely as it will be used in later chapters to determine the feasibility of your ideas.

Table 2.1
Personal Goal Guide

GOALS

Income needed	Personal satisfaction objectives	Self-esteem considerations
	(rank from 1 to 5)	*(rank from 1 to 4)*
$ _____ year 1	_____ recognition by others	_____ status in community
$ _____ year 2	_____ helping others	_____ personal growth
$ _____ year 3	_____ expressing creativity	_____ expertise
	_____ developing expertise	_____ other
	_____ other	

Table 2.1
Personal Goal Guide *(continued)*

TYPE OF WORK DESIRED

Type of activity	People contact	Business involvement
(rank from 1 to 6)	*(rank from 1 to 5)*	*(rank from 1 to 5)*
_____ sales	_____ direct customer contact	_____ part-time
_____ technology	_____ indirect customer contact	_____ 40 hrs/wk
_____ working w/hands	_____ work alone	_____ 10-12 hrs/day
_____ working outdoors	_____ work closely w/suppliers	_____ weekends only
_____ administrative	_____ work closely w/personnel	_____ absentee owner
_____ other (specify)		

LIFESTYLE CONSIDERATIONS

Travel	Entertaining	Community involvement
_____ yes	_____ yes	_____ yes
_____ no	_____ no	_____ no
_____ limited	_____ limited	_____ limited

Acquired abilities (specialized [languages, software], general [management, sales]): _____

_____

_____

Personal capabilities (or limitations): _____

_____

_____

Risk tolerance: Give consideration as to how great a risk taker you are. How much internal anxiety do you feel when taking a chance?

(circle one)   High   Moderate   Low

Financial capabilities. It is necessary at this point to recognize the financial limitation that may be imposed. Refer to table 2.2 below to estimate the money available for a small business start-up. Raising additional capital will be discussed in chapters 6 and 14. However, there must be recognition of what you are able to contribute personally. Neither banks nor investors will offer assistance if the entrepreneur is not confident enough in the idea to risk their own money. There is a definite correlation between amount invested and the time it takes to get a business off the ground. A $10,000 personal investment rarely correlates with a million-dollar-revenue business. The profit-to-investment ratio varies greatly by industry; however, using a 20 percent annual return on investment is a fairly conservative guideline. For example a business that requires a $100,000 investment should be able to return $20,000 to the investor after all salaries, including the entrepreneur's, and taxes are accounted for.

Table 2.2
Determining Personal Capital Available

Assets		Liabilities	
Cash on hand	$ _____	Outstanding bills	$ _____
Stocks/bonds	$ _____	Bank notes	$ _____
Other securities	$ _____	Other notes payable	$ _____
Accounts receivable	$ _____	Credit card debts	$ _____
Real estate; home	$ _____	Home mortgage	$ _____
Other real estate	$ _____	Other mortgage	$ _____
Life insurance cash value	$ _____	Automobile notes	$ _____
Personal belongings	$ _____	Other debts	$ _____
Automobile(s)	$ _____		
Total Assets	**$** _____	**Total Liabilities**	**$** _____

NET WORTH CALCULATIONS

Total assets	$ _____
Less total liabilities	$ _____
= Personal net worth	$ _____
Liquid assets available to invest	$ _____
Amount of capital willing to invest	$ _____

It is extremely important to subtract out the assets that are liquid and available for investment as opposed to those that are not. Unless there are personal belongings (i.e., collections) that you are willing to sell, do not list them as available. This is normally true regarding cars, as you will need transportation. We will discuss how some assets can be used as loan collateral, that is, real estate or securities, in a later chapter. You will need to determine how much of what you have you would be willing to invest in recognition of the risk factor of a business enterprise.

Do not be discouraged at this point in regard to personal financial capabilities as there are ways (to be discussed later) to improve the situation, but be realistic enough to recognize any outlandish ideas.

Does the Idea Fit the Profile?

Venture ideas come from the following.

Personal experience. Most new businesses arise from an individual's past experience and the feeling that they can do it better. The restaurant manager who opens her own restaurant to compete against her former employer; the fashion designer who after years in the industry has found a willing investor to support her new designs; the hair stylist who persuades her regular customers to follow her to her new shop are all examples of this. Dave Thomas, the founder of Wendy's Restaurants, opened his first Wendy's after years of working in a Kentucky Fried Chicken franchise. It is the most common and best road to success. As pointed out in the profile, use the assets you have accrued. The experience and contacts developed over years of employment can help immensely in the start-up phase of a business. Examine your capabilities and assets and then look closely at business opportunities that allow you to use them.

Accidental discovery. There are times in all of our lives that we stumble upon an idea and exclaim "someone should make this and take it to market." It might take the form of a new kitchen utensil, a garden tool, a game, or in the case of a young father, a way of getting his kids out of a jam. Tim overheard his wife telling his sons, age 7 and 11, to pick up the baseball cards off the floor or else she would throw them away. This hit home as he recalled his childhood baseball card collection and similar threats from his mom. For all he knew she might have done exactly that as he never knew how his collection had disappeared these many years later. With that in mind, he and his sons took a green poster board, drew a baseball diamond on it, placed the cards in plastic pockets and attached them according to position and hung it on their bedroom wall. In a matter of days neighborhood kids were asking Tim if he could make them one. It spawned an entrepreneurial thought and before long he and a friend were manufacturing and selling with success baseball card plaques. There are many such stories, some with phenomenal success (remember Pet Rocks?) If you are harboring such an idea consider taking it to the next step.

Hobbies. Imagine taking a hobby, something you love to do, and turning it into a commercial enterprise—the ideal business that should certainly pass the profile test, Unfortunately it is not always practical, but not necessarily impossible. A young lady in Knoxville, Tennessee, enjoyed creating costume jewelry pieces in her spare time and giving them as gifts. A friend who sold fashion apparel offered to take some samples to an apparel trade show and put them on display. She came back with orders in excess of $25,000. The jewelry creator never looked backed and within a year hired workers and a staff (including her husband) to help control her growing business.

Deliberate search. If the determination is there but not the idea, embark on an extensive search to fulfill a community or industry need. Research various markets of interest. If you want to open a shoe store, find a market that needs a shoe store. Don't do this without full demographic research, as first impressions are often incorrect. Go to industry sources to learn the per capita income needed for a product, how much population is needed per outlet, age of preferred customers, desired educational level, and so on. Such a project will take effort but the rewards will warrant the task

Idea Evaluation Questions

In addition to matching your idea to your personal profile, examine it as to the following 10 questions.

1. What kind of business can this venture become in the short run and the long run?
2. Why does the opportunity for this venture exist?
3. Who will be the first customer and why can that person be expected to buy?
4. What will make it possible for this business to withstand competition when it comes?
5. Are there others who are in a better position to accomplish this venture?
6. What in the rank order are the three most critical assumptions upon which the success of this venture is projected?
7. What is the upside potential of the business if things go as well as can reasonably be hoped?
8. What is the likely downside loss if things go unfavorably?
9. What has to happen for break-even to occur?
10. How sensitive are the projections to key variables in the environment?

The Creative Process

Creative ideas for a business opportunity usually follow a path to success. An early American psychologist, Graham Wallas, identified the following steps:

Interest ("Hmmm"—look around)
   Preparation ("What now?"—collect information)
      Incubation ("Maybe?"—step back and mull over)
         Illumination ("Aha"—feel the excitement)
            Verification ("It will work"—all indicators are positive)
               Exploitation ("Success"—take it successfully to the market)

Identify where you are in this process.

Lastly, Why Are You Doing This?

I have been laid off and can't find work. Not a good reason by itself.

I have been alerted to an opportunity by a friend. Friends do not necessarily qualify as personal advisers.

I just received an unexpected windfall of money. Might work if the idea has not evolved strictly from the windfall.

I have worked in an industry long enough to learn the ropes and see an unsatisfied need. Bingo: now you are making sense.

My research has shown that my hobby has commercial appeal, particularly in regard to new technology. Could be perfect.

I have performed extended market research into finding an underdeveloped market in my locale. Maybe, but why haven't others moved on this idea?

I have an invention. Great, but is it marketable and have you researched the cost of patenting and bringing a new product to market?

My friends are encouraging me to make more of what I make and sell to retailers. There are often good products that do not make good businesses. If it takes you an hour to make the product, how will you make 100 per day in order to make a profit? Probably by hiring and training many people and investing heavily in production equipment. Investigate thoroughly.

Chapter Story: Unrealistic Expectations

The following scenario points out the dangers of assuming "greener pastures" without taking an account of what is important to you. Perceptions are often exaggerated as we fall prey to hearing what we want to hear and seeing what we want to see. Your perceptions are developed around knowledge. The more you know, the more accurate are your perceptions. If you do not take the time to properly learn about possible opportunities, your perceptions can be very misleading, as evidenced in this case study.

"I'll tell you Jim, I have paid the price for my success." Bill was chatting seriously over drinks with his best friend. "I am the CEO for a big company and have never made so much money, but I am too exhausted to enjoy it. Except for weekends I have been home only three nights in the past month. That's a typical month. I have lost touch with my family and friends. My job has evolved into a PR job—all I seem to do is travel and make speeches. Success may be great for the ego, but what about the soul? I envy you owning your own small business and being in control of your own timetable. I don't need the money as much as I need to slow down. I need your opinion on a business opportunity. It's a chain of six laundromats here in the metro area. It sounds great to me—look at these numbers."

Jim and Bill reviewed the income statement that showed a business that earned a $100,000 annual profit before the owner's draw for salary. The selling price was $150,000. Bill had figured that he could cut his present income to $70,000 per year, which would allow a $30,000 annual payback on the original $150,000 investment, a 20 percent annual return on his investment. Projected growth would allow him to return to his present income level in a year. "I really want this, Jim. I would not have to travel. I could spend part of each day in my home office and the other part out checking on locations. It's ideal. Each store has its own manager, so if I want to take a trip with the family or play golf, I will be free to do so. I can open additional outlets to generate more profits. I will be able to control my own destiny. No more corporate world. I am ready to write the seller a check; what do you think?"

Jim was scratching his head in consternation. "Bill, I think you need to slow it down a bit. I don't believe it is quite the scenario you are expecting. Believe me, I have owned businesses for fifteen years and it's harder than you think. I don't know the laundromat business, but I can guarantee you there will be some unexpected surprises."

"Aw, come on Jim, this is a piece of cake compared to what I have been working with. You are just spoiled. I am going ahead with it"

The company was shocked at Bill's resignation. There were goodbye parties, gifts, and a genuine display of sorrow. Bill was deeply touched and had, at times, some fleeting second thoughts.

Jim proved to be right. What Bill expected and what he received were far different. It was not a "piece of cake." The maintenance of equipment alone was a nightmare. He spent many afternoons surrounded by pieces of washing machines and dryers. In addition, store managers were constantly asking for higher pay, not showing up for work, or quitting without notice. He did not realize that controlling an expense budget for a small business was just as challenging as a large business. The difference was that every added expense was coming from his already reduced salary. His first attempt at opening an additional outlet was a shock as well because he did not realize it took an average of eighteen months to build a profitable customer base.

Worst of all, he missed his old company. He missed being treated and looked upon as a CEO. The travel, the speeches, the people, and fast-paced lifestyle had become part of his routine and he missed them. The promised utopia of his return to family and more family trips was less than expected, as he was afraid to leave the business for any extended periods of time. The headaches of his new career were just as tiring as the old ones.

"Why" he thought, "couldn't I have just done a better job controlling and balancing my previous job; after all, I was the CEO."

Closing Tip

List ten rewarding life experiences and explain why they were rewarding. Was it because you solved a problem, made a new friend, received a bonus, received recognition for community service? Correlate the reasons with your VANE and see if they match what you have proclaimed to be the priorities in your life.

3

The Challenges
and Prerequisites

THERE ARE SOME PREREQUISITES FOR BECOMING SUCCESSFUL ENTREPRENEURS. Not everyone is prepared to enter the world of self-employment. As cited, approximately 60 percent of start-ups do not last past five years. Some fail because of market changes, others because of personal difficulties—illness, divorce, and so on. Many fail simply because the founder was not equipped to withstand the problems encountered. Consider the following before proceeding.

Personal Characteristics

A very essential personal characteristic is self-confidence. You will get knocked around, particularly in the early stages. To handle these times you need to believe in yourself and your idea. If the conviction going in is not strong, back off. Confidence teamed with determination will carry you through the tough times.

A second characteristic is creativity. Being creative does not mean being the next Steve Jobs, it means outthinking your competition. The winner will be the one who does it the best with the most flair. No one is asking that you be the best in the world; just being the best in your marketplace will do fine.

The third is the thirst for self-actualization—the strong desire to feel the thrill of victory. You need to be the type of individual who once a goal is achieved is ready to move on to the next.

Of course there are other recommendations that can be cited, such as coming from a family of entrepreneurs or having a fat billfold, but these are secondary if you possess the three just mentioned.

When

Timing may be critical. Are you ready, and is the market ready for you? The present mood of the twenty-first-century economy is not overly optimistic, but that may not be a reason to shelve the idea. It is a good time to be conservative in your outlook and forecast. Keep in mind that bad economy or not, there are still unsatisfied needs in the marketplace; some are just hibernating. It also means that the competition is not as strong, meaning there is more potential opportunity. Many of the businesses that have failed did so because they were not strong enough to stand up to the times. Other businesses will come along and take their place—why not yours? Being conservative in fragile times does not mean giving up on your idea, but it may mean taking a different approach. Since borrowing money is harder, think smaller. Getting your feet wet with a part-time venture might be the direction to go. Or find a partner to share the risk. Or consider a franchise that is doing well in spite of the times. Or buy an established business. Or do a more thorough job of researching your market and find more windows to open to enlarge your market. If you wait for the perfect time, your idea may just stay an idea until you are eighty years old and sitting on your porch wishing you had given it a shot.

Risk tolerance

How are you equipped to tolerate risk? If you cringe with every fluctuation in the stock market or when you hear a dire economic forecast, you need to be careful in what venture you pursue. Risk correlates with profit. The greater the risk normally means the greater the profit potential. Bringing an untried product to market is risky, but if it catches on the reward will be substantial. Buying a very established franchise or business is not as risky and its profit potential will be more in line with how much is invested versus how much risk is taken. The middle road is buying into a business or franchise that is on the threshold of great success. Even the best-known franchises had their early days of growth and distribution. The early franchisees made great investments, much better than those buying into the same franchise twenty years later. Look for franchises that are regionally successful but getting ready to go national. Or look for a business for sale that has a solid foundation but only lacks the creativity or ambition that you can bring to its future.

Three Ways to Pursue Your Dream

Taking all the preceding into consideration, you need to determine the best way for you to enter entrepreneurship. You can buy an established business, you can buy into a franchise, or you can start a business from scratch. Your choice will be determined by a number of factors—opportunity, finances, and risk tolerance.

BUYING AN ESTABLISHED BUSINESS

This should be your starting place regardless of the direction you believe holds the greatest opportunity. Why? Because by investigating the business for sale's market you will learn much about your idea and possibly about your competition. In particular, if the business that is for sale is in your marketplace, the information is invaluable. It will give you a firsthand look at what sells and what doesn't, what to expect down the road, what suppliers are dependable, who is the most fierce competition, and what are the market trends. You will be given the opportunity to peer into the books and history of a business much like the one that you will operate. And, under the right circumstances, you just might buy it.

Buying an established, successful business is ideal for those who tend towards having a security anchor. There is a track record, suppliers are in place, and trained employees may be part of the package. It becomes a turn-key opportunity—little guesswork and plenty of time to learn. But make sure it is a successful business opportunity. The majority of businesses for sale are not good opportunities. They are on a downward trend with poor management. Look at the sales trend, review the books for accuracy, don't make assumptions. The seller may say they are selling due to retirement, illness, new opportunities, and so on—none will say because the business is falling apart. It is your job to determine the real reason and get a grasp on the potential of the business for the future.

The ideal opportunity is one which only lacks your input to be successful. It may need capital to push it to the next level, better management to control costs and identify opportunities, or a new spirit of enthusiasm. It is a business that borders on the brink of greater success, just needing that missing ingredient that you can bring to the table. Its past is good, although maybe showing signs of stagnation, its equipment and inventory are up-to-date, it has good relationships with its vendors, and a solid community and customer image. The price might be higher than what you expect, but you can negotiate, and there is the possibility the seller will hold a note for a significant part of the purchase price, thus eliminating the banker as an obstacle to your goal. Negotiating and gaining a seller's note will be a good test for your entrepreneurial spirit. When the seller holds the note, it is secured by the business. If things do not pan out, the seller takes back the business, so he or she is quite invested in your future; therefore, you gain a valuable ally who can be of great help to you at the beginning of your new career.

HOW MUCH IS IT WORTH?

There are three factors to review to determine a business value.

Replacement Value

If the business is relatively new it should be relatively easy to obtain an assessment for the value of the inventory, equipment, and leasehold improvements (the property improvements). This allows you to compare its value to the cost of you putting the business together yourself. It does not account for the value of goodwill that has been created by a nicely run operation or the added advantages discussed above and that can be considerable. It also does not account for the value of the location. Determining the replacement value is a good negotiation tool, but left by itself it is limited.

Liquidity Value

How much could you receive from the sale of the business on an emergency basis? What would liquidators give you for the inventory and equipment? This is not a pleasant thought, but it happens. You will need to discuss this with industry sources who buy surplus inventory or used equipment to obtain a value.

Market Value

What have similar types of businesses in similar markets sold for in the recent past? The best place to get this information is from the industry. Visit trade shows or call industry vendors to see what you can discover. This is certainly not a science, as all markets differ, but it can be a helpful guideline in your considerations

Return on Investment

This is the big one. The factors listed above are in the mix, but the bottom line is how profitable will this business be in the future and how that can be determined. You know the "for sale price" and you have a history to project from. If you have done due diligence in making sure that the figures supplied to you are accurate and you have a plan for the future of how your abilities can benefit the business, you can go to work in determining whether it is a good investment. One rule of thumb that is pretty accurate is to make sure you are receiving a 20 percent return on the money invested. Compared to the current securities market, 20 percent is very good; however, the risk and effort involved in owning and operating a business are also greater. In simpler terms you should be able to recoup your initial investment after being paid for your efforts in five years. If you were to buy a business for $100,000 you should be able to confidently expect to receive approximately $20,000 per year (not counting a fair personal salary) payback on the $100,000. That may be in the form of paying back $20,000 per year on a 5-year $100,000 loan used for the purpose of purchasing the business.

Your challenge is to realistically project your sales and profits over a five-year span. Start with the seller's past year results and conservatively add what your management and expertise can add to the picture. Keep in mind that your ownership will not change things overnight, but should make a significant difference over a longer period of time. Figure 3.1 illustrates such a method.

Figure 3.1
Projecting a Business Takeover

INCOME STATEMENT PROJECTED ADJUSTMENTS FOR FIRST YEAR

	Actual [past year]	New owner plans	Projected
Sales/revenues	$300,000	Should be able to increase 10%	$330,000
Less cost of goods	160,000	Increase inventory by $20K	195,000
Gross profit	140,000		135,000
Operating expenses			
Payroll	$60,000	Eliminate one employee	$45,000
Rent	24,000		24,000
Utilities	3,000		3,000
Maintenance	2,000	Add new lighting	2,600
Insurance	2,800	Additional inventory coverage	3,000
Accounting	2,400	Keep own books	500
Advertising	3,000	New promotions	4,000
Supplies	4,200	More sales = more supplies	4,800
Miscellaneous	4,000	New incidentals	5,000
Total oper. expenses	**$105,400**	**Projected 1st year expenses**	**$91,900**
Net operating profit	**$ 34,600**		**$43,100**

Bottom line, if a realistic projection over five years does not recoup your investment, move on to the next opportunity but take what you have learned about this business with you.

Often the very best opportunity is buying an established business in which the owner is willing to hold a note on any unpaid balance after a down payment. This eliminates the bank, which is good and injects the previous owner's experience and advice as he or she will be dependent on your success in order to receive the remainder of the money owed. In this instance the collateral is the business itself. If the buyer defaults, the seller assumes ownership of the business. If business turns bad, the buyer might be quite willing to relinquish ownership back to the seller. If business goes well, the buyer will be able to settle the debt and sometimes pay a lower rate of interest than a loan from the bank. It is always a good idea to inquire if the seller is willing to sell on agreeable terms. The seller in this case will receive a regular monthly or quarterly income and possibly a tax break on capital gains.

There are pros and cons to buying business for sale opportunities:

Advantages	*Disadvantages*
No business start-up expenses	Could inherit obsolete inventory
Suppliers are in place	Could have bad supplier relationships
Employees are in place	Employees could be poorly trained
Customer base created	Poor reputation will need time to repair

Franchise opportunities

Franchising has certainly boomed over the past forty years and has worked to the favor of many entrepreneurs. For the inexperienced business owner, it provides a path to almost immediate experience. The franchisee (buyer) buys into a network of established business procedures and hopefully a recognizable trade name. The franchisor (parent company) creates a very fast way to expand their venture. It can be win-win for both, but it is not without its risks.

Not all franchises are successful. As a matter of fact, there are many fly-by-night operations acting as franchises. Any business can franchise if they can find franchisees. If you start a successful business you might someday wish to sell the rights to use your trade name and business operation to another person in exchange for a down payment and a royalty agreement that is based on a percentage of sales. It is a quick method to expand while using another party's capital instead of your own or going into debt. This might be particularly true in fast-moving, competitive markets in which timing is critical and a novel idea might be duplicated, such as the fast food industry. For this reason there are predators whose greed can lead them to over exaggeration of the facts. Review the following list of advantages and disadvantages and see how they match your entrepreneurial base and VANE.

FRANCHISING ADVANTAGES

- The franchisee receives an established product or service.
- In most cases the franchisee receives management assistance and training.
- Consumer acceptance is based on consistency and familiarity.
- Operating expenses are often less due to franchisor quantity purchasing power.
- In some cases the franchisor may help with the financing or provide valuable support on obtaining bank financing.

FRANCHISING DISADVANTAGES

- A continuous payment contract to the franchisor in the form of royalties to be paid on revenues.
- Limitations in regard to what products or services the franchisee can offer.
- Procedures and regulations will inhibit the independence of the franchisee's decision making.
- Dependence on the franchisor for future reputation and quality of service and product.
- Overdependence on the franchisor in regard to management assistance and termination of franchise agreement.

In consideration of any franchise agreement, the potential franchisee ought to seek legal counsel. There are franchise laws that protect the franchisee that are overseen by the Federal Trade Commission; however, they are often violated. Of particular importance are regulations regarding financial and legal disclosure on the part of the franchisor. It is imperative that the true financial status of the franchisor be open for inspection and that all legal actions brought against the franchisor be clearly explained. Protected territory complaints, fraudulent representations, and hidden fees are not uncommon in the franchise world. The prospective franchisee should take the initiative in contacting other franchise owners and not just the ones the franchisor recommends.

Successful franchising investment is often a result of timing. In seeking a very established and successful franchise the entrepreneur will pay more as risk is reduced. These types of franchises are ideal for the stability-based entrepreneur. On the other hand, the challenge and creativity-based entrepreneur will not be happy with a franchise unless they are on the ground floor and can participate in the growth of the franchise network. If a franchisee can join a relatively new franchise the investment can be very rewarding and exciting. The early McDonald or Pizza Hut franchisees are certainly now living the good life. The prospective franchisee should be on the lookout for a growing, well-managed regional franchise that has not expanded nationally but has plans to do so in the next three to five years.

The cost of joining a franchise is as variable as the types of franchises. The normal procedure is to pay a franchise fee up front. This covers the acquisition cost of the business and its assets and its goodwill. Also included in this is the cost of training the new franchisee. In addition there will be ongoing costs, usually in the form of royalties depending on sales and often an advertising surcharge. The franchisor may also act as the vendor for supplies and inventory. In this case buying a franchise can be attractive as the franchisor may have quantity purchasing power that obtains lower prices than what the independent business owner can get. Be careful not to accept an original sales pitch of owning a franchise for, say, $10,000 as there may be much more associated with the purchase than the initial franchise fee.

There will be a direct correlation between the success and stability of a franchise opportunity and its cost. A new franchise might very well cost $10,000 (the original Subway franchises cost $6,000) as opposed to an established franchise trade name such as Pizza Hut, which may cost several hundreds of thousands of dollars. Many franchisors will offer a financing plan to assist, but usually only after a hefty down payment.

Starting from Scratch

Okay, you challenge and creativity entrepreneurs, this is your arena. Starting from scratch and building a business is exciting, very challenging, dangerous, and rewarding. Starting a business on your own is particularly pertinent if:

- The entrepreneur wishes to avoid the dependence, interference, and policy-setting dictates of a franchise.
- The entrepreneur does not wish to assume the poor precedents of an existing business.
- The entrepreneur has developed a new product or service that has not been marketed before.
- The entrepreneur has found an ideal location and has the support of bankers or investors and suppliers.
- The entrepreneur has gained sufficient expertise and experience from his or her previous job that it is time to test their abilities against the competition.

Going out on your own takes the willingness to assume risks and a special ingredient of marketing savvy. The successful entrepreneur has a special gift of marketing his or her product in a manner different or better than anyone else in their marketplace. There is one very essential prerequisite; the aspiring entrepreneur must be willing and able to write a business plan.

Your Personal Business Plan

Creating a business plan means creating a map to follow that will lead you to goal attainment. You must do it. Many of the 60 percent of the businesses that close in their first five years are started on impulse with little or no research. There is little in life that you can accomplish without planning. Ideas are easy, but implementing them can be very challenging. Do not deny yourself a map to follow—research and learn before leaping. A properly written business plan clarifies and validates your proposed venture.

Take the challenge as if you are writing a short story. Make it personal; after all, it is your dream. Write out your goals and how you are going to attain them. At first it can be very loose but eventually it will tighten up. Soon it will take shape and you will show it to people. First your family to assure them that you have not gone crazy, and later possibly to investors, bankers, or family/friend sponsors. In some fashion it needs to address all the ingredients of a business plan.

INGREDIENTS OF A BUSINESS PLAN

The business plan should be comprised of eight sections.

The general business description. Start with a general description of the type of business, its primary product, and its intended market. It should address why the particular type of business was chosen and why it should be successful. It is very important to point out to the reader why this business is better than the competition—its competitive advantage. Sketch out answers to the following questions and then write them out in a narrative format.

- What is the business?
- What market do you intend to serve?
- What will be your competitive advantage?
- What are your short-term and long-term goals?
- What will be your operating schedule?
- What talents do you bring to this business?

The market analysis. This is the research part of the plan. Using demographic data, it should identify the total market potential for the product or service and clearly identify your target market—your strongest customer base. Also address the competition, the choice of location, and any economic constraints or potential in this section.

- How big is the total market?
- What is the target market?
- What share of the market can the business attain?
- Who is the competition? What are their weaknesses? Strengths?
- Where and why was the location chosen?

The information needed will come from both primary (original) and secondary (published) sources. The primary information may come from interviews and surveys of potential customers and suppliers while the secondary demographic information will require visits to the library and other research facilities.

The marketing strategy. The emphasis of this section is to explain how the business will attract, satisfy, and keep its customers. It should address advertising and sales strategies. This section should also include pricing strategies.

- How will the business attract customers?
- How will the business satisfy and keep customers?
- What advertising strategies and media will be employed? Include website, domain, and social networking strategies?
- What sales and promotion strategies will be employed?
- What pricing policy? Why?
- What will be the credit policies?

The management plan. The management section of your business plan should identify all ownership entities and cite the experiences and competencies of each. Explain the roles of all key personnel and when applicable show an organization chart. Address what control tools will be utilized, that is, an accounting system, software applications, insurance plans, inventory systems. Describe suppliers, manufacturing processes, if applicable, and equipment required.

- Who are the owners? Managers?
- What are their backgrounds?
- Who will do what?
- What control tools are in place?
- How will the business operate?

The legal plan. You will need to check out any legal requirements that will affect the business. Any special licenses or regulations need to be researched. The choice of ownership structure—sole proprietorship, partnership, LLC company, corporation—needs to be identified and defended in regard to tax and liability considerations. Any important contractual relationships should be clearly explained.

- What licenses are needed?
- What contracts need to be reviewed?
- What form of ownership works best?

The financial plan. The financial plan should explain the expected outcome of money invested or loaned to the business entity. This is accomplished through the use of pro forma (projected) financial statements (income statements, balance sheets, cash flow statements) for at least the first three years. Both short-term and long-term financial needs should be clearly stated. A confident assertion assuring that a proper return on investment or loans will be attained. A break-even analysis should also be included.

- How much money is needed?
- What will happen to that money?
- What is the financial projection?
- What is the plan to attract investors or lenders?
- What is the contingency plan?
- What is the break-even plan?

Supporting documents. Any supplementary materials which will add credence to the business plan should be an appendix to the report. This may include personal resumes, letters of intent from potential customers, brochures, menus, and so on.

Executive summary. Although this is the last part written, it is the first section of the business plan because its intent is to sell the reader on the viability of the business. It is often thought of as the opening statement of a sales presentation. Its purpose is to motivate the reader to continue to read.

- Why read this?
- What causes the reader to get excited?
- What is the potential?
- What is needed to reach the objectives?
- Why will the business be profitable?

Writing the business plan may be the first test of how strong your resolve is to be an entrepreneur. It will take time and research. Be realistic and build an information network. If you are not willing to write and research a business plan, you are not ready to be an entrepreneur.

Chapter Story: Reality Check, the Long Road to Success

If you have never owned a business or been exposed to business ownership through your upbringing, it is important to get a grasp on what the normal curve to success might entail. The story below follows Joshua and provides some insight into what it is like to own a business.

Joshua did not like his office job or the corporate world. He did not like the routine, the rules, or the boss who would question his arrival time when it was 8:05 A.M. He wanted independence, challenge, and growth.

His first answer was to switch jobs. He found a sales position with a large greeting card company that gave him much more autonomy. He set his own schedule, worked out of his home, and saw his boss once a week. It was better, but after a couple of years similar problems arose. Unannounced sales meetings, unrealistic sales quotas, and a very demanding boss started to take their toll. The boss was a drinker and a womanizer who would go to great lengths to achieve the district sales goals. Joshua called on retail outlets. He started thinking that maybe instead of worrying about fifty accounts, he might be happier worrying about one—his own.

There was no doubt that Joshua had the right background. He had learned a lot about the industry after selling for three years. He was a people-oriented person who was not afraid of long retail hours. He had enough confidence in himself to assume a reasonable risk and make decisions. His age, twenty-nine, was a plus factor as he was not tied into any pension plans or sending children through college. His desire led to an opportunity. A card and gift shop that was suffering in an economically depressed town was available on favorable terms. The seller would hold a three-year note for $75,000 of the $100,000 selling price.

YEAR 1

Joshua was the proud owner of a business with its operations and employees in place. The new young boss inherited a staff of four older women, three of whom had been employed for over five years. Some had to go to make room for Joshua and his wife. Firing people was new to Joshua and he quickly found it to be very difficult. Being a mall store, the hours were seven days a week and twelve hours per day. When Joshua wasn't there he was constantly calling to make sure all was okay. There was much more to it than smiling to customers as he completed a sale. There were fixtures to be moved, trucks to be unloaded, and stockroom work. At the end of many days his back hurt from moving furniture, his feet hurt from standing, and his clothes would be dirty from unpacking shipments. But . . . he loved it because it was his own business.

The change in lifestyle was dramatic. Joshua quickly realized that the challenge of controlling even a small business was a much larger responsibility than being on a company payroll. Joshua's duties were all-encompassing and ranged from cleaning the bathrooms to creating ad copy for newspaper and radio. All decisions came to him, no matter how trivial. The real challenge was creating a cohesive working unit with his employees. He learned the best way to do this was through sharing. Therefore, he made sure that socialization was a central part of the organization. Parties, wedding, showers, and luncheons with employees all became part of his new lifestyle. He also realized that as a community retailer it was important to be recognizable so he joined the local Rotary Club, the Chamber of Commerce, and sponsored youth events.

A typical workday for Joshua might start with a Chamber of Commerce or Rotary breakfast meeting before arriving at his store at 9 A.M. to prepare for a 10 A.M. opening.

The mornings would consist of a staff meeting, UPS deliveries, and check-in of merchandise and changing displays. Lunch was more than likely a sandwich at his desk which was frequently interrupted by customers needing assistance. After lunch a possible truck delivery of maybe 30–50 cartons might arrive and had to be unloaded and unpacked, leaving Joshua's clean shirt a wrinkled mess.

On evenings that he would work, usually two or three per week, he would return at 7 P.M. after having arrived home after five to have dinner with his family. If he was not working at night, his wife probably was, and he would stay home with the kids. Slow days were spent on bookkeeping chores, merchandise ordering, and planning marketing activities.

It was the busiest year of Joshua's life and not the most lucrative. He and his family had to make the changes necessary to live their lives around a business. This included being overly tired and missing some paychecks due to poor cash flow. Many poor decisions were made during that first year and the debt payments were very difficult to handle. However, after a stagnant start the business started to show some significant growth gains and community acceptance was much higher than the previous owner had attained.

Year number two started with optimism and a low checking account balance.

YEAR 2

Although year 2 was not as hectic with change, Joshua's association with the business intensified as the challenges continued to mount. Desire to succeed reinforced his perseverance. There were times that Joshua had to make a conscious effort to stay away from his store in order not to lose sight of other important things in his life. If he took an afternoon off to play golf, he would work the evening shift in order not to miss a day's contribution. It was still a one-person leadership situation; the only vacations were an occasional long weekend.

Although the business was still as consuming as ever, it was not quite as exhausting since the operation was becoming more predictable. Since everyone now knew what to expect, more order came to Joshua's and his family's life. The personality of the business became recognizable. There was a growing feel of loyalty and camaraderie among the employees. Joshua felt he was gaining control of the situation. The sales momentum continued to the point that the debt payments were becoming manageable, and although still far from his previous salary in the corporate world there was improvement. Joshua was able to envision that the day would come that he could expand his operation.

YEAR 3

Business continued to grow and debt started to ebb. A true sense of confidence developed within Joshua and the dream of expanding was becoming a reality. It was exciting. He investigated opportunities whenever they came his way. At one point he even considered buying out an old family-owned department store in the neighboring county. There were those who told him he was reaching too far too soon, but Joshua had that entrepreneurial gleam in his eye.

When the department store possibility did not pan out, Joshua started laying out a business plan that would expand his present operation three-fold. New departments would require a larger facility, additional staff, and increased risk. However, they also offered a potential 400 percent sales and profit increase. Joshua had finally reached a time of some stability and was now considering jumping right back into the fire. But wasn't that the point? New challenge and greater profit achievement would bring goal fulfillment and a better standard of living for his family. It would also create jobs. Was it worth the risk? Would his family support another gamble? He was learning that to get to the brass ring, you had to reach as far as you could without falling off the horse.

THE EPILOGUE

The family and the bank supported Joshua's dream. The business did expand and did so successfully. During the following years Joshua lived his entrepreneurial lifestyle and kept to his creativity entrepreneurial base. The excitement was always there, the risk ever-present, but he was a very satisfied individual. He provided well for his family and was envied by his friends. Living on the edge had its difficult times but became a way of life. Joshua looked back on those first three years and sometimes wondered how they ever survived. But they did survive and the ends certainly proved worthy of the means.

Closing Tip

Be realistic in your goals. Rarely does success come overnight. It takes patience and tolerance and that is why you need to make sure that you are in the right environment. Joshua was successful because he knew what he was getting into, he wrote a business plan, and he stayed within his entrepreneurial base and personal profile.

- Review your personal characteristics as they relate to entrepreneurship
- Investigate all possibilities
- Write a business plan

AND

MAKE SURE YOU HAVE THE SUPPORT OF YOUR FAMILY

4

Finding Your Selling Comfort Zone

SELLING IS THE LIFEBLOOD OF ANY BUSINESS. WITHOUT SALES, THERE WILL BE no profit, and profit is the food for business survival. Whether or not the idea of selling appeals to you, it comes with the title of entrepreneur. You must know how to sell your product or service if you are to be successful. But before moving on, take the time to think through some rather commonsense viewpoints of sales and make sure you feel comfortable selling the product or service that your business idea represents. With practice, selling a product or service that matches your VANE will come naturally. If you must convince yourself that the product is something you believe in, the chances of success are almost nil.

The Essential Elements of Successful Selling

What is your first memory of selling? Elementary school sales contests for the PTA, the front yard lemonade stand, the church bazaar? Actually you have been selling since you were a youngster, whether selling your mom on wanting more dessert or to stay up later. Some carried this ability through their school years in part-time jobs, or in earning money by getting lawn mowing or babysitting jobs. What have you learned from past sales experiences? With these and other sales experiences in mind, let's take a simple but very relevant look at the three basic beliefs an entrepreneur needs to possess to be successful as a salesperson

#1 BELIEF AND KNOWLEDGE IN THE PRODUCT OR SERVICE

To be successful you must believe in your product or service. If you believe in your product you will know that you are satisfying a customer's unsatisfied needs, thus helping them. Helping someone by selling them a product or service they need is not difficult.

You must understand the term *product;* it is much more than the tangible item or final service delivered. The product is the total bundle of satisfiers your business and product represent. These satisfiers include the packaging, the customer service, the guarantee, and the exchange value that is offered. Understanding all elements of the product will allow the entrepreneur to gain repeat sales. Selling a product one time will seldom get you to your goal. It will be achieved through repeat sales over the long term. Your sales philosophy must show the confidence that the product will deliver in all areas, not just one or two. This is why we go back to preaching the importance of choosing the right business. You cannot be successful selling with reservation. If you do not have confidence that your product is right for a particular customer it will show. The entire sales group of the business has to share the same belief in the product or service.

Confidence comes through knowledge. The more you know about your product, the more confidence gained. Product knowledge should provide an appreciation for its qualities. Take the time to study what you sell. If it is food, learn culinary arts, if computer equipment, learn about its capabilities. If fashions, become active with the fashion industry and learn what will serve your customer the best. The knowledge and enthusiasm the entrepreneur has for the product or service must be transmitted to the entire sales team. They will want to learn and you must provide the learning vehicle and materials.

If you believe in what you are doing, selling will become natural and fun. Helping people make the right decision to satisfy a particular need will bring you personal satisfaction.

#2 BELIEF IN THE FEATURES, ADVANTAGES, AND BENEFITS OF THE PRODUCT AND HOW TO APPLY THE BASIC SELLING STEPS

FAB stands for features, advantages, and benefits that a product or service represents. What is the FAB of your chosen business?

The *features* are the characteristics of the product or service. What does it appear to be? This includes its size, packaging, color, flavor, price, service, shape, uses, and ingredients. Citing the features of the product tells what it is. Features attract but do not sell. They do not tell how it is used or specifically what need it satisfies. For a tangible product they are clearly announced physical characteristics; for a service they are clearly implied. What are the features of the product or service you are considering? Make sure it will do all that is stated or implied before moving on—your reputation stands on how the product lives up to its features.

The *advantages* are the performance characteristics of what is being offered. How fast does the computer operate, how clear are the camera's photos, how healthy is the food, are examples of advantages. You and your salespeople must be able to describe the advantages to the point where the customer can mentally visualize its performance. Your business represents how the product performs or the service is delivered. If it fails to live up to its advantages, customers will be disappointed in the value exchange and will not return unless it's to request a refund. Make sure that you have tested in every possible manner how the proposed product or service that your business represents lives up to its advantage statements.

Benefits are the result of the advantages. The most important element to the product or service is what it will do for the customer. What need is it satisfying? The customer very simply wants to know "what's in it for me?" If you cannot answer that confidently with great belief, you are in the wrong business. People buy benefits, while the features and advantages attract and support. In the long run value is measured by benefits.

As an example let's use a quick-mix food product. Its features might be: made fresh from natural ingredients, only needs water, stir and cook. Its advantages include great taste, nutritious, and easy to prepare. The benefits would be saves time, more time with family, attractive appearance.

Combining all three in proper sequence is part of sales training, but knowing the elements of each is imperative to your success. Do the features, advantages, and benefits of your intended venture match the values, attitude, needs, and expectations stated in your personal profile as stated in chapter 2? If they do you will easily put together a sales program consisting of the following:

Proper approach: An engaging welcome designed to open communication about your product.

Convincing presentation: A well-planned recital of the features, advantages, and benefits your business has to offer.

Confident handling of objections and concerns: Then proper application of your knowledge to answer questions and defend your presentation

Correctly closing the sale: Asking for action is crucial, but not difficult, if the preceding steps have been carefully implemented. The close should be created around the benefits of the product or service.

Follow-up: Good business use follow-up as a method of ensuring customer satisfaction and gaining repeat sales.

#3 BELIEF IN THE GOLDEN RULE TO SELLING

It should be obvious but is often not followed: *sell unto others as you wish to be sold.* Put yourself in the place of the customer. Show the customer the respect and kindness that you would expect and that customer will become a repeat customer. It is the imperative rule to becoming a successful business owner. Relate the benefits of the product or service honestly to the needs of the customer. It should come easily to the owner, but what about the sales associates? Will they be trained to adhere to the rule or will they stray away from it for an extra commission when no one is looking ? Our society is confronted daily with barrages of stories of unethical sales practices. Often there is a correlation between the size of the business and the number of violations, for example, Walmart. As businesses grow they become more vulnerable to unscrupulous conduct. They lose their way often because the owner/founder is not present to uphold the original values of the organization. They are managed by agents representing the ownership, not the owners themselves. Small businesses have a distinct advantage here. They are more personable, cooperative, and flexible and this is why they will always exist and why a segment of customers prefers to buy from them. You will find that strong customer relationships will determine your sales growth. The good owner puts in place sales policies that ensure the customer is always treated fairly; these sales policies adhere to the "golden rule."

Different Types of Selling for Different Types of Businesses

The type of business you choose will determine the type of sales program you follow.

RETAILING

Retailing and service businesses are ordinarily a softer sale than manufacturing or wholesaling businesses. The customer comes to the retailer, which means he or she has a definite need or they would not be there. There is no need to establish that there is a need, which makes the path easier. Selling in this instance requires arousing enthusiasm and confidence that the product will satisfy the unsatisfied need. The biggest obstacle is competition. There are many businesses to choose from. Why did the customer come to yours? Was it convenience, product selection, reputation, price, service, or all the above? When they leave how will they feel about the business? Will their attitude be positive? Retail operations often require long hours.

SERVICE SELLING

Service businesses depend on credibility. Are you the best plumber, accountant, auto mechanic, or graphic artist? Consequently, selling means proving oneself. Over time the business will build a reputation, but initially the service provider will need to sell their background, experience, or education. It is a soft sale but it requires confidence and communication skills.

It is not enough just to hang a shingle out with your name on it. Selling comes through doing. Sometimes by discounting services initially, leading seminars, or doing demonstrations at public events. Very simply selling services means selling yourself. This requires a strong entrepreneurial base of self-confidence. The service provider is often subject to being on call at inconvenient times.

MANUFACTURING AND WHOLESALING

A manufacturer or wholesaler, however, is faced with prospecting, and at times cold calling, which requires identifying that there is a need, a much more difficult assignment. Prospecting is finding qualified customers who have an unsatisfied need. It is often a long and arduous assignment in which some may not wish to engage, somewhat similar to that door-knocking you might have done in selling PTA raffle tickets or Girl Scout cookies. If you choose this type of endeavor you will most likely be selling in trade shows or at the client's place of business. Trade shows are fun and exhilarating but can be tiring and sometimes very difficult. A trade show may have hundreds if not thousands of exhibitors selling to a multitude of attendees. Rows of displays and sales booths will be competing for the attention of the walk-by customers. Once established, repeating customers will seek you out, but initially you will need to be discovered. Attractive displays and giveaways are techniques employed. This is not the place for the timid entrepreneur. Product knowledge is essential as often customers are looking for tools they need for their own business and they are quite knowledgeable. Providing sufficient information, verbally and in handout printed materials to the customer, is a requirement. Manufacturing and wholesaling sales requires travel.

If still deciding on a venture, consider the type of sales that you will be doing. In consideration, keep in mind that the retailer has long hours, the service provider is on call, and the manufacturing and wholesaling ventures will most likely do some traveling.

Testing Your Sales Aptitude

Dale Carnegie has long been considered the father of successful selling. His book, *How to Win Friends and Influence People,* was written in 1937 and is still used as the basis for sales training in 400 of Fortune's 500 largest businesses in the world. Almost eighty years later Carnegie's words of communication are recited at sales meetings on a daily basis across the globe. Let's review some of these principles and see how you measure up to them. Following these principles will provide you with the foundation for success in your business venture.

Don't criticize. Trying to correct a person only arouses their defenses—a no-win for your business. Criticizing a customer as to their opinion or behavior will leave a bad taste and lose a repeat sale.

Give sincere appreciation. Phoniness will show through. There is always a positive element in any situation—find it. Don't flatter just to flatter.

Arouse an eager want. This is good salesmanship. You believe in your product; convey that belief into a sale.

Display your interest in the other person. Carnegie points out the greatest winner of friends in the world. The tail-wagging dog that will jump out of his skin to tell you how much he loves you. Let your customers know how much you care for them.

Smile. It says so much and can lead to so much good.

Remember names. We love to be recognized and hate to be forgotten. Learn memory techniques, keep databases—whatever method that works for you. Take it a step further and keep track of birthdays, anniversaries, and so on.

Be a good listener. Listening is a skill that many do not develop. It requires effort. We like to talk too much about ourselves and not let the other person talk. Listening to customers first before presenting information allows you to understand their needs.

Make the other person feel important. This is an outcome of listening.

Avoid arguing. Even if you win you will lose a customer. A customer who spends $100 and comes back once a year for 20 years has a value of $2,000. Don't argue over one $100 purchase; it may cost you $1,900.

Admit that you are wrong. Self-pride will defeat you in the long run. Tell customers when you make mistakes, apologize—you are human, they are human.

Get the other person to say yes. This is a universal law of effective salesmanship. Saying yes leads to saying yes, so get the yes response from the beginning. Salespeople are trained not to lead with questions like "May I help you?" that can elicit a negative response. Positive to positive, negative to negative.

Let the other person feel like the idea is theirs. This is always good strategy and a way of making the customer have confidence in their decision. Lead but don't decide for the customer.

See things from the other person's viewpoint. Step back, put yourself in their situation, find points of agreement.

Dramatize when applicable. Dramatization creates excitement, and is a good tool for creating enthusiasm.

Apply challenges to those around you. Competition can be good. Selling can be made into a game. A game your sales associates will enjoy if rewarded for success.

Be an effective leader of your sales team by using praise and encouragement; asking questions as opposed to giving direct orders; admitting to your mistakes before criticizing your associates; and always letting the other person save face by only calling attention to people's mistakes indirectly.

If you are comfortable with these lessons—GREAT! If they arouse reservations, get thee to the bookstore or library and purchase Dale Carnegie lessons.

Consumer Psychology 101

If you are going to be a successful entrepreneur you will have to apply what you have learned in your psychology lessons. Just as important as understanding your values, attitudes, needs, and expectations (VANE), you will need to understand the needs, perceptions, attitudes, and motivations of your customers.

Needs. Needs are much more broadly defined than most believe. Needs in regard to consumer psychology are those things, tangible and intangible, that are required to maintain a person's standard of living. Therefore needs differ depending on an individual's standard of living. An expensive designer shirt may seem a frivolous want to some, but to a teenager whose friends are wearing this look it will appear as a need to stay included with the in crowd. You may have studied Maslow's Hierarchy of Needs in a psych course. Dr. Maslow explained five levels of needs and how we move up the need hierarchy after we satisfy needs at the previous level.

Figure 4.1

Maslow's Hierarchy of Needs Pyramid

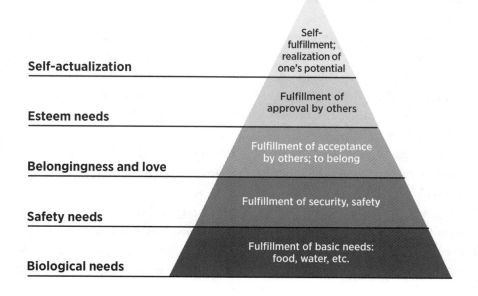

Entrepreneurs must be aware of the need level that they are selling to or take the chance of losing a customer. An example would be a car salesman approaching a customer regarding the purchase of a new car. If the customer is looking for basic transportation to get to work and visit friends and family it is a different need level than the customer looking to purchase a new luxury car because he or she recently received a promotion and raise. The former is looking to satisfy a belonging need. The car allows that person to get to work or social events that are important to their circumstances and being part of society. The latter is looking for a reward for achievement. The new luxury car will satisfy self-esteem and possible self-actualization needs. The salesperson who tries to sell a self-esteem purchase to a person desiring a belonging need will fail. The lesson: study your target market and make sure you are familiar with the needs that your product will satisfy and how those might differ among your customers.

Perceptions. Our perceptions are the way we view and understand things. They are determined largely due to our backgrounds and the amount of information and knowledge we possess about particular subjects or about a business's products, services, and reputation. Perceptions become ingrained and they play a significant role in how we make purchase decisions. This is why strong favorable brand identification is so important to large corporations. The same holds true for small business in regard to their reputation and products offered. By providing accurate information with good products and service we enhance the perception of the business and it will be viewed favorably. The favorable perception creates a favorable attitude regarding your business.

Attitudes. A customer's attitude is how he or she feels about a certain product or service. Attitude is a derivative of perception. Is it favorable or unfavorable? The reason large companies spend so much money on advertising is to create a favorable attitude toward their brand. If the entrepreneur is selling a well-known brand name such as Hallmark or Vera Bradley they rely on the company's marketing efforts to create the positive attitude to their product. In this case it will be up to the entrepreneur to uphold that image. If the entrepreneur is selling their own product without the support of a recognizable brand name, the consumer's positive attitude must be instilled through their purchase and use experience

Motivations. Motivations are the reasons we take action. To persuade a customer into action, the entrepreneur must give them a reason. Exposing unsatisfied needs creates tensions within us which give us the motivation to act to fulfill the need. A fashionably dressed mannequin can create a need for a new outfit which in turn may create a tension that will only be satisfied with a purchase. The better you understand your target market the easier it is to motivate them. This is where marketing strategies discussed in chapters 7 and 12 come into play. However, successful marketing techniques cannot be achieved without creating the positive perception and understanding what needs you wish to arouse.

Assisting with Decision Making

Do you enjoy helping others make decisions? Successful selling requires assisting others in making a decision. Your choice of ventures will dictate how extensive this process may be. In situations that are complicated and not routine, the consumer will require much encouragement and assistance. Some goods, called convenience goods, are relatively free of decision making and are almost habitual. The assistance may come in the form of a colorful display or convenient location. Other decisions will require more effort from the entrepreneur. In particular are specialty goods that may be expensive or very complex due to technology. A purchase decision such as deciding on a new fashion purchase is comprised of several steps in which the entrepreneur can play an important role.

1. **Recognize the need.** A mannequin displaying a new fashion may arouse the need for a new look.
2. **Analyze the cause of the need.** The customer may be thinking of an upcoming social event. Surround the display with color and an event setting.
3. **Review alternatives to relieve the need.** The customer may be thinking of possibly mixing and matching what the customer already owns to create the new look or borrow an outfit from a friend. The entrepreneur is offering a great price that enhances the exchange value.
4. **Select from the desired alternatives.** Good personal selling.

5. **Make the exchange transaction.** Make the exchange as easy as possible by accepting credit cards, offering a layaway plan, and so on.
6. **Evaluate the purchase.** Prevent buyer's remorse with attractive packaging, a discount coupon available for the next purchase, and a sincere goodbye and please come back.

Successful entrepreneurs take an active role in leading potential customers through the decision-making process. They understand the value of various marketing stimuli to expose the need and cite the cause. They understand the customer's anxieties and tensions and the need to review alternatives. They provide information that will give confidence to the purchaser. They are also aware of cognitive dissonance—the feeling of uncertainty as to whether the purchase decision was the right decision—and they will follow the sale with a compliment, phone call, or possibly a letter conveying a positive attitude regarding the benefits of the purchase and a sincere expression of appreciation and support.

Training Others

Entrepreneurs not only act as business owners and psychologist but teachers as well. You will quickly find out that you do not have the resources of the big boys in regard to hiring and training. In many instances you will be hiring unskilled workers and training them yourself on the job. This is not always bad because the best person to train someone is the owner of the business. However, the training will only be as good as you make it, and in sales work training is extremely important. The trainer must not only teach the product and process, but also transfer the enthusiasm for the product or service to the student. As mentioned, you will be a good salesperson because you believe in the product and the business. Your challenge is to channel that belief through your salespeople.

Too often small business owners fall prey to thinking that no one can sell their products as well as they can. This causes a delegation problem and leads to micromanaging the sales force. Success will come by providing freedom of expression to salespeople once they have acquired the necessary product knowledge and understand the fundamental steps of the selling process.

It will take patience and in some cases tolerance. Do not expect a new person to be capable of doing all facets of a job in a few days or even a few weeks. Sales training should start with learning sessions regarding the product. In many cases there may be videos and literature from suppliers to share. The new associate should be assigned initially to you to mentor, and at a later date to another associate if available. They will need to learn not only about the product but the customers as well. The selling process can be taught in role-playing situations and is often supplemented with a sales training course or books such as the Dale Carnegie book. After viewing a number of sales situations as an observer, the associate should be free to leave the nest, but only after the entrepreneur feels he or she will do an admirable job of representing the business. Keep in mind that salespeople are representing you and you do not want to make a bad impression. Do not hurry this process.

Chapter Story: The Wrong Sales Technique

The following scenario recounts the story of not matching the proper sales technique to a company's customer base. In this case the owner acted out of panic and did not think through either the customers' needs or the needs of his own sales force.

George was disappointed in the sales reports laying on his desk. All three of his salespeople were selling below expectations. Although the number of sales calls had increased, the dollar results were below the previous quarter. He wondered whether the new sales strategy he had introduced four months ago was backfiring.

The new strategy was the result of George being impressed by a speaker he had heard at a sales convention. The speaker discussed "selling to the max" in a very motivational presentation. The theme was one of not relenting when selling. His philosophy was the more you ask for, the more you sell.

The lesson was not to give up and not to take no for an answer. Persistence pays off.

The timing of the speech was appropriate as the packaging industry like so many others was in the throes of a slump. The healthy sales increases of a few years back had come to a screeching halt. George had been pondering what he could do to get more from his sales force. They too had been disappointed as their commissions had become stagnant. Maybe, thought George, they needed to push harder.

In presenting the new sales philosophy to the sales force, George received a lukewarm reception. His plan was to increase the number of sales calls per clients, offer price reductions for immediate delivery of certain size orders, and remind customers of the expense of handling small orders. From the results on his desk it was apparent the new plan was not working. He called in Dick, his top salesperson, for some feedback.

"George, we feel like used car salespeople at times and hatchet people at other times. We are not used to selling deals. We used to sell pride in product. The idea of inferring that we might not be able to accept small orders is insulting to our regular customers. Some have been glad to remind us of how those small orders have added up over the years. Add to that the extra sales calls and it is apparent we are gaining resentment, not sales."

George knew Dick was right. What had he been thinking?

Closing Tip

How a business sells is a reflection on the owner. Stand by your VANE and understand your customer before determining your sales philosophy. It has to fit your product, your customer, and most importantly, you.

5

Narrowing Your Choices

S O FAR THE DISCUSSION HAS BEEN ABOUT FINDING YOUR DIRECTION. NOW let's look where this information may guide you by reviewing five general categories of business opportunities:

Retailing has many platforms from which to choose: retail storefront, Internet selling, restaurateurs, vending machines, network marketing, and many part-time operations.

Professional services range from certified and licensed occupations to home improvement services.

Wholesaling can be as simple as arranging product transfers or as complex as being an international importer and global marketer.

Manufacturing can be as a subcontractor or possibly as the inventor of a product; there are many opportunities in all industries.

Part-time business ownership is often the best way to get started or a very valid option for the semi-retired or stay-at-home parent.

There are some very important considerations that should apply in choosing any small business. Michael Porter, a well-known business strategist and theorist, stated there are three paths to establishing a business in a very competitive market. Your product or service must be strong in one of the three:

1. **Be a price leader.** Low cost drives customers. Can your business compete with the large businesses? Probably not. Chapter 10 will demonstrate the dangers to small businesses of discounting.
2. **Offer a unique product or service.** This does not mean totally original but one with distinction that is not what is termed a "convenience" product. Adding good customer relations to a "specialty" product will allow your business to compete against all competition.
3. **Offer a highly focused product or service.** This niche classification represents the unusual that cannot easily be found or duplicated (see the case study at the end of this chapter). Such products and services are often difficult to find but, if available, this strategy can provide security and success.

Retailing

STOREFRONT RETAILING

For many generations mom and pop retail stores accounted for the greatest number of small business owners. However, the door for successful independent retailers has closed substantially. The superstores and corporate America have firmly grabbed the dollars of retail store shopping. Look around at your local shopping centers and malls. They pretty much look the same—all dominated by national chains. Many retail stores are now owned by the companies that used to wholesale their products to the mom and pops. Certainly the opportunity window has narrowed but not totally closed if you have the creativity, personality, and location that will allow you to outfox the big boys. Creative entrepreneurial-based individuals with managerial aptitude can prosper.

Pros

If you have an energetic, enthusiastic, and outgoing personality you will love retailing. Every day you will interact extensively with the public. Your customers will become your friends. Your staff will become your teammates. There are never two days alike.

The creative entrepreneurial base individual thrives in an environment of constantly meeting the challenge of outdoing the competition with creative merchandising, product selection, and marketing schemes.

Although the rate of return of investment is often long (usually 3–5 years), once achieved the retailer is on the way to a potentially lucrative career that can grow at whatever pace the entrepreneur is comfortable. Profit range for an independent retailer can run 15–20 percent of revenues. A couple of $500,000-volume stores will quickly build your nest egg. It might also allow you to pass the business along to children or sell for a very rewarding profit when it is time to move on to something else or retire. Another caveat is the possibility that the day may come that you can act as an absentee owner/manager and just stop in occasionally after a round of golf or check in by phone from an exotic vacation spot.

Cons

Yes, the hours are long. Store hours will normally range from 48 hours per week to 84 depending on where the store is located, and that does not include opening and closing chores. The new owner will feel compelled to be present for the majority of those hours. The good news is that as experience and staff training take hold it will get easier. But long hours and standing on your feet is the life of the storefront retailer.

The investment is usually quite high and the return on that investment will not happen overnight. Inventory is only part of the opening cost. Capital is also needed for store decorating (referred to as leasehold improvements), display fixtures, cash register, and stockroom equipment. For example, a new store with projected sales of $500,000 may need an initial opening inventory investment of $50,000–$100,000 and probably an equal investment in the above mentioned leasehold improvements.

Risk can be high, particularly if discounters and national chains are nearby that carry similar products. The key to success in contemporary retailing is uniqueness and personal service. Trying to compete head on with discounters will lead to failure, so make sure your store offers that something different.

Managing a Retail Store Operation

Managing a retail store requires administrative and human resource skills. The owner will need to develop an inventory control system that assures the proper amount and selection of goods are available at all times. Software programs for inventory and financial controls have been of great assistance, but they still require discipline to maintain.

Just as important is the ability to handle personnel matters with staff and customers. A poorly trained sales staff is evident and will be the undoing of a business that is based on customer relations. Independent retail stores may not be able to compete with the chain store operations in regard to capital, but they can bury the competition in regard to customer service. It is their strong point. To be successful the environment must be warm and knowledgeable. This all starts with the owner and filters down. It is not an environment for individuals who are not people-oriented or who are poor communicators.

Lifestyle and Other Considerations

The store retailer's lifestyle will revolve around the store; however, he or she can control which of the long hours they choose to work. The work environment is friendly with much interaction with people. Every day is different, and there will be many hours spent with salespeople at the store or working with vendors at trade shows. The large merchandise trade shows can be fun. The buyers are exposed to thousands of product lines and in many instances entertainment by vendors. As a buyer, trade show days are long but offer a change of environment as buyers congregate in the larger metropolitan cities to see what is new in the marketplace. Also keep in mind that as a community store owner it will benefit your business to be active in the community. Retailers should consider Chamber of Commerce, association, and service club organizations. In addition, there will be many requests to support local charitable causes and youth organizations.

Challenge/independent and creativity entrepreneurial-based entrepreneurs are ideal candidates for this choice. It requires strong values, an optimistic attitude, a firm understanding of the needs of others as well as their own, and a very realistic sense of expectations.

INTERNET RETAILING

You may recall the quote from *The Sound of Music,* "when God closes a door, he opens a window." That quote pretty much describes the role that Internet retailing has played for the retail entrepreneur. When the opportunities for independent retail stores began to be taken over by the large discounters and national chains, many independent retailers turned to the Internet. It holds less risk because it requires less investment.

Pros

Once the right niche is found the Internet retail business is quite simple to operate. The retailer will, in most cases, line up with an Internet hosting service that will transmit the order to the entrepreneur, take the payment information, and in some cases handle the payment transaction. The business owner will receive orders via e-mail. Normally these orders will be forwarded to the owner's e-mail address by the host company and will provide all details of the order, including shipping address and payment information, usually credit card payment. An e-mail will automatically be sent to the buyer notifying them that the transaction is in process. The owner simply packages up the item and hands it over to a delivery service.

The investment and operating cost are smaller than a storefront operation. There is no need for expensive leasehold improvements, personnel needs are less, and the owner does not work by a clock. Except for possible storage space there will not be a lease. The phone and the computer take the place of a store.

To many it is the ultimate freedom. There are no dress rules for working out of your home office and no posted hours. The owner has total control over the business. There is still the excitement of finding the right product. Creativity is involved in product selection and website display. There is some customer contact, but certainly not to the degree of the storefront.

Cons

The competitive marketplace for Internet marketing gains in intensity every day with more and more entries. It requires a highly focused product to compete for attention. Buyers are guided by the ranking of sellers under search engines. The more you are willing to pay, the higher the ranking. A highly niched product such as glass etched art may be able to gain a superior ranking for $.25 per click while a bed and breakfast inn might spend $1.25 per click-through to its website. Google is the number one search engine but there are others as well, and the savvy Internet seller should be active in many. Since your budget will not allow you to outbid Walmart or Amazon for priority search engine listing, it is better to avoid their arena and go with products that they do not sell. A unique product description allows a business to be listed higher at a fraction of the cost of a more generic product description. A listing such as model airplanes will go against hundreds while a listing for World War II model planes will have considerably less competition.

Website design is getting very sophisticated. Originally the marketer could show some nice photos and text and pretty much do it themselves. Contemporary websites are loaded with movement, music, videos, and so on and often require the services of website design firms. Web design professionals charge fees comparable to accounting firms. A well-developed website may cost $2,000–$5,000 to create. Since you are selling products there is a constant need to update and replace products. Taking some web design courses can eliminate some of the dependency on the professional website firm and save you a good bit of money.

It is not as simple as keeping a website up-to-date. The Internet retailer has the same inventory control challenge as the storefront retailer. Hopefully dependable suppliers can be found to deliver fast and cut down on inventory storage. Logistical movement of shipping goods to customers will have to be found. This will include learning packaging techniques.

Lifestyle and Other Considerations

The challenge/independence and creative entrepreneurial-based entrepreneurs are also very well suited for Internet retailing; however, a technical base can also find satisfaction. The lifestyle is one of freedom but also requires discipline because working out of a home office will offer temptations to stray from the tasks at hand. You can skip the community involvement if it does not fit. Check closely your personal satisfaction needs before proceeding because the isolation factor can be threatening.

It can get lonely. Normally these businesses are operated from a home office and it may be manned by just the owner and his or her dog or cat. Many will miss the water cooler fraternity and personal interaction with customers.

RESTAURATEURS

This is one of the most competitive industries of them all. Many restaurants are here today and gone tomorrow. The reason is the fickle customer base and the fads that rule the industry. The successful restaurateur will take on all challengers and once firmly established will become a pillar of the community.

Pros

If you survive, it is a wonderful life, particularly for outgoing people. You will become a town favorite. Constantly meeting and greeting people and providing them with good food and sometimes entertainment is a fun occupation. Creating new dishes is a creativity stimulus. There are so many innovative marketing paths to follow in establishing a restaurant that every day is distinct. The profit that comes from a proven restaurant is very high. Food profit margins are high, and if you serve alcoholic beverages the profit margins are even greater. If not satisfied with owning one establishment, the door is open to expand into more—maybe even franchise your operation.

The path to success needs a disciplined guideline to follow. One young lady named Kate graduated from a prestigious college only to accept a restaurant waitress and receptionist position at the restaurant she had worked for during her college years. This came as a surprise to her fellow graduates who were boasting of their high-paying corporate entry jobs. Fifteen years passed by as our restaurateur learned the ropes and then opened her own upscale restaurant with great success and profits. Now her old college friends often stop by for an expensive dinner and complain, "I am so tired of corporate politics and demands, I sure wish I had done what you did."

Cons
New competition seems to pop up on a weekly basis. It seems like everyone who has a great recipe would love to take it to the marketplace. Most are not suited for the challenge or the daily grind. Long hours filled with multiple crises are daily. Equipment failures, employees who do not show, and irritable customers are commonplace. Food spoilage and health inspectors are also part of the restaurateur's life.

The staff training function is challenging. It is not enough to hire personnel with a great smile. Restaurant operators are dependent on strong staff members to help with menu selection, food appearance, inventory maintenance, tip calculation, and many other daily operations of the restaurant. It is a good idea to join the American Restaurant Association for guidance in staff training and customer relations.

Restaurant hours are very long and last into the evening. The restaurateur seldom has evenings at home with the family and social adjustments will be necessary. Check your personal profile closely. Also beware of friends and family believing they merit special treatment in regard to costs.

Lifestyle and Other Considerations
If you have a strong challenge entrepreneurial base with a strong sense of perseverance and can match the restaurateur lifestyle to your career profile, you might be a match for this exciting occupation.

Don't be fooled into thinking that because you are a good cook, you should own a restaurant. Offshoots from a full-time restaurant operation include bakeries, sandwich shops, or ice cream parlors. These specialty food services will often be more suitable for many.

PROFESSIONAL SERVICES
Let's define professional services as any occupation that requires a certain amount of training and often certification to enter the field. Therefore the range is from plumber to doctor. People often do not consider doctors, law-

yers, artists, and so on as entrepreneurs, but they are if they have hung out a shingle and are out on their own fending for a living.

Pros

Recognition, praise, and high profits come to the best. Almost everyone in the community can cite the best automobile mechanic, builder, or doctor. If the entrepreneur achieves this type of recognition he or she can rest assured that jobs and profits will keep coming their way. The good service provider is not afraid to request high fees because they are the best and their work will outlast the competition and in the long run be a greater value.

Finding the right customer base for your service can go a long way to building success. Jim, an air conditioning service provider, was an avid baseball fan who owned a marginally profitable business which primarily serviced middle-class homes. He was a fan of the Atlanta Braves and bought good season tickets each year. One year his season tickets happened to be next to those of a wealthy banker who lived in the elite Buckhead area of Atlanta. During the long season they became baseball buddies. In the course of conversation, the banker expressed concern for his home air conditioning maintenance provider. He accepted Jim's offer to inspect his system at no charge. The inspection resulted in Jim installing a new system in the banker's 10,000-square-foot mansion. It wasn't long before Jim started to receive service requests from the banker's network of wealthy friends. Jim's business soared from marginally profitable to highly lucrative as a result of finding a better customer base.

Cons

In addition to time spent developing the necessary skills either formally or through apprenticeship training at low pay, the service provider needs to build credibility. This is often done by word of mouth and satisfying one customer at a time. There is no quick road to success. There will be the expense of setting up the service, ranging from equipment to tools or necessary supplies.

Be careful not to enter an oversaturated marketplace because there is only room for so many offering a particular type of service. Also be aware that a poor economy and new technology can be a constant threat to many service providers.

Lifestyle and Other Considerations

The lifestyle of the service provider may be hectic in that often you are on call at all times. A locksmith enjoying a Sunday afternoon at home may be called out to assist a traveler in crisis due to locking their keys in their car. This applies as well to realtors, doctors, plumbers, and many other service providers. Anxiety can also be high as these occupations are driven by perfectionism and not every incident works to perfection.

Expertise entrepreneurial-based individuals should be guided into professional service work. This is their haven in that they will have the opportunity to work on developing their skills to the level desired. In addition, service-based entrepreneurs are often included in this occupation. They manage community services and must gain the necessary psychological and administrative skills to lead such organizations

SMALL MANUFACTURERS AND DOMESTIC AND INTERNATIONAL DISTRIBUTORS

Are you an effective coordinator, negotiator, and time manager? Manufacturing and distributing products (wholesaling) demand these abilities. A small business owner who engages in a business-to-business type of business will have more control over business operations than many other entrepreneurs. They control operations at the ground level. The economy benefits from these businesses as they create jobs.

Pros

The manufacturing/distribution businesses provide a truly independent work occupation. The business owner controls all aspects of the business from product creation to final delivery. There is no passing the buck; it is all yours.

Selling has a different challenge than retail. Sales calls to clients will often require travel and sometimes entertaining by dining out. You will live by a calendar of appointments. Your clients will become your friends as over time there will grow a mutual dependence and trust. Trade shows are great for meeting and opening new accounts. As an exhibitor you will need to arrive a day early to the show in order to set up your display and be the last to leave after take-down. The shows are fun and exciting but also very tiring because you will spend the day on your feet selling and the evenings often entertaining clients. The larger the show the more expensive. In addition to travel and lodging expenses, booth space rental will be costly, often $500–$1,000 per day.

When it is time to get out, the successful manufacturer/distributor should have no problem finding buyers. Industries are like private clubs in that the successful members are well known and respected. A successful business will sell for many times its investment and can lead to a very satisfactory retirement.

Cons

China and other low-labor-cost countries have invaded American production and distribution arenas. Many have been forced to close operations or else utilize these markets to gain a competitive price. It is a much more complicated marketplace than in previous generations.

There is a high dependence on suppliers in this occupation. The delivery of materials needed for production of products to be shipped to retail customers cannot be late. There must be contingency plans in place for any breakdown in the system or important customers will be lost. Business owners must constantly work on building solid relationships with their vendors to receive priority treatment. Paying a supplier late will cause disruption and be costly.

Pleasing the customer may mean working overtime to get an order out. Uncertain working times and conditions should be anticipated. A strong quality control system is mandatory.

Setting up production and storage space will be costly. Outfitting a manufacturing business with the necessary tools and equipment will normally require a significant outlay of capital. It is important that the equipment uses current technology and is updated on a regular basis. Storing large quantities of goods as a distributor requires warehouse and office facilities. Location also becomes critical as it may determine how timely you can deliver shipments or the time spent traveling to clients. Insurance cost may be high if there is risk of work accidents.

Lifestyle and Other Considerations

Due to the diversity of functions, a manufacturer or distributor will need assistance from staff or family. It is an excellent business to employ and pass on to family members. There is also room for expansion into new product lines and new markets, including international ones. International businesses used to be only for the big businesses, but that has changed dramatically. Over 50 percent of new small businesses now engage in some types of international activities. Often they start with limited exporting to or importing from neighboring Canada or Mexico but then grow to South America, Europe, and the Far and Middle East. Trade treaties and ease of currency exchange have made the transition easier, and the profit potential is unlimited. Globalization adds excitement and adventure. U.S. businesses are represented at trade shows throughout the world. For assistance in entering foreign markets, contact an office of the Department of Commerce and International Trade. Our government is very interested in expanding U.S. exports in order to cut into our trade deficit and will provide great assistance to the small business owner.

The manufacturer or distributor is a fit for most entrepreneurial bases including expertise. Many will prefer it over retailing because personal interactions are more narrow and focus on clients as opposed to the general populace.

THE PART-TIME ENTREPRENEUR

For many of the readers of this book, part-time business may be the best way to go. There are approximately 10,000,000 part-time entrepreneurs operating businesses in the United States. Many operate from their home, garage, or workshop. Part-time businesses are becoming increasingly popular with the early baby boomer retirees as a way of staying active and supplementing their retirement budgets.

Pros

For those opening a business on a tight shoestring, it gives time to develop a business while still employed and receiving a regular paycheck. It takes time to build a customer base; a part-time endeavor can provide that time.

Operating a business on a part-time basis allows the entrepreneur to gain experience. There are always beginner mistakes, but the mistakes will not be as costly if the entrepreneur is still on someone else's payroll.

A part-time business is a great way to turn a hobby or field of interest into a business. If successful, the entrepreneur is guaranteed job satisfaction.

If operating a business from a home office, workshop, or garage the owner is entitled to some generous tax advantages. Providing the area is distinctly used for business, the owner may deduct a portion of housing and utility cost. The home computer and supplies become a business computer eligible to be declared as a tax-deductible business expense. The family car when used for business purposes will be allowed to have that portion of its upkeep declared as tax deductible. Operating a business from home saves on taxes and eliminates the overhead expense of rent. If at all possible, starting a business at home is advisable. The business owner can wait to have the fancy office or more elaborate work space after the business is well established.

Cons

By its very nature, being a part-time business implies secondary priority. Priority will still be with one's full-time occupation. There is a constant challenge to maintain vigilance over the business while still working a regular job.

Working a business after work hours or during usual leisure times will become tiring and will require discipline. There will be times when you feel you are never off work. The motivation must be strong, which is why it must be an endeavor that you truly enjoy.

Family activities may suffer, particularly in the home-based business. You will need the family's support to allow you at times to remove yourself from family obligations in order to pursue your goal. If you conduct business from a home office, it needs to be separated from family activities. Clients do not wish to contend with barking dogs or loud children while discussing a possible order over the telephone. It is always a good idea that whenever possible you involve the family with the business. This will allow them to better understand your goals and often provides a team approach to share in the problems and successes.

As in a full-time business, a part-time business will still require that the entrepreneur write a full business plan. There is no substitute for research and planning. Keep in mind that the more information you have the less risk you will encounter. There are hundreds of ideas from which to choose. Use your creativity instincts and make a list of potential ideas. Some crazy ideas have worked. One gentleman advertised trading fishing lures. For $1 plus postage he would exchange one of his lucky lures with one of yours. Basically he was just exchanging one customer's lure for another at no cost to himself and did quite well. The following is a list of fifteen part-time endeavors to get you thinking; there are many more.

1. **Internet retailing.** This may start with eBay and grow into an exciting full-time occupation.
2. **Pet sitting.** Possibly start with some neighborhood dogs and then reach out to the community. Ten pets per day at $30 each is not bad as long as you enjoy pets. You might also include the service of caring for your clients' homes when they are on vacation.
3. **Flea markets.** Spend your weekends at the local flea market selling your goods and those of others. Eventually you might expand to larger flea markets.
4. **Crafts.** What do you enjoy making? The craft market has a sizable following through local craft shows. Pack up your SUV and rent a booth and see what happens. Not only might you make some money, but many enjoy the camaraderie of these shows among the many interesting vendors.
5. **Novelty button making.** Someone makes all those team, school, and club buttons—why not you? All it takes is some pretty simple machinery (Internet search "button making machines") and a very minable investment (less than $500) and you are in business.
6. **T-shirt printing.** This is similar to button making but somewhat more complex and requires a larger investment. T-shirt printing can lead to wholesaling to clothing stores or setting up your own storefront, particularly if you are in a tourist area.

7. **Children's party catering.** Today's dual career families seldom have time to create the child's entire birthday event. You can coordinate the entertainment, party decorations, food, and birthday cake.

8. **Wedding planner.** A step up from the children party catering and more demanding but at a higher fee. Start with helping a friend and graduate to advertising your services.

9. **Janitorial service.** Not glamorous but can be profitable. Start with a small local commercial office building and clean 2–3 times per week.

10. **Lawn/home maintenance.** Maybe you mowed lawns as a kid—why not as an adult on a larger scale? Large yards need help, and with the right equipment you can handle as many as you wish. If you are in a vacation area take care of second homes for owners who are only part-time residents. By the way, your fees are much higher than when you quickly mowed a lawn as a teenager.

11. **Tutoring services.** Help the frustrated parent with the education dilemma. What was your best subject in school? Bone up on it and seek tutoring clients. Not just the 3 Rs of school subjects but also swimming, tennis, archery lessons, and so on.

12. **Desktop publishing.** Professional printing services are costly and often do not fit the small business's or nonprofit organization's budget. If you are competent at your computer photo cropping and writing script, you can fill a need at less cost than the local printer.

13. **Video memories.** If you have good video equipment and develop the expertise, there is a market for creating family video auto-biographies. A grandparent telling his or her stories on a CD makes a wonderful gift to the family.

14. **Mobile pet grooming.** Many pet owners prefer not to leave their beloved pet in a cage at a pet salon. They are willing to pay extra for a pet groomer to come to their home. Buy the clippers and after many hours of practice, let the word out that you are available.

15. **Freelance writing.** Prepare articles on subjects that you have knowl-edge about and send them out to newspaper and magazine pub-

lishers. Get your leads from writer magazines or *The Writers Market,* a reference book for writers—available at your local library.

The list can be easily expanded—house painting, mailing services, firewood selling, pamphlet distribution, home organizing, and so on. What unsatisfied need exists in your community?

Lifestyle and Other Considerations

Part-time business ownership is available to all entrepreneurial bases, although some will desire to expand into a full-time operation faster than others. If you have an idea, give it a try. There are too many who are sitting on their porches wishing they had given it a try. It's more fun than watching television in your spare time. Even the stability base should not be afraid to tackle such an ambition. A part-time business requires a smaller investment and thus less risk.

A Look At The Real World: A Part-Time Business Grows Up

"Honey, where did you buy this ship in a bottle model?" Steve was contemplating starting a collection from the gift his wife Susan had given him for their anniversary the previous summer. "I found it in that nautical gift shop we visited in Maine last summer," Susan replied.

Little did Steve know that this simple question was to lead him into the life of an entrepreneur. A call to the store to purchase another received an out-of-service recording. A rather extensive search for another store that sold ships in bottle models proved unsuccessful. An Internet search followed also to no success. He found souvenir models but nothing of the handcrafted quality that he sought. The question rose in his mind "Am I the only person in the United States who finds these models to be of interest? I can't be." Finally Steve found a source, a German craftsman from Hamburg named Johann, who operated a family business crafting and selling the models throughout Europe. E-mails followed starting with an inquiry if Johann would sell Steve a model and ending with a discussion as to whether Steve would have an interest in being the U.S. distributor for Johann. Before he knew it, Johann was visiting Steve in his home in Georgia and a business plan was hatched and created that set up Steve as both a U.S. wholesaler and Internet retailer of European Crafted Ships in Bottles.

In its origin it was a part-time operation working from Steve's basement from which he stored inventory and shipped products to online customers. It continued in that manner for over a year until Steve took a big step by renting a trade show booth at the Atlanta merchandise mart to exhibit his products to thousands of retail store buyers. Bingo! Over sixty stores made a purchase and the days of a part-time endeavor were behind him.

Many challenges were ahead. A more professional website was developed, the additional inventory purchase required renting outside shipping and storage space, wholesale brochures were designed and printed, computer hardware and software were upgraded—all of which added up to a significant additional investment. The initial investment of $2,000 for inventory now stood at $25,000, which required some borrowing. Steve was no longer filling orders on a leisurely basis but now spending time marketing, traveling to retail accounts, and staying on top of his Internet sales as well. In addition, as an importer Steve had to learn customs procedures. Susan was brought in to help and eventually an additional staff position was created.

The business continued to grow in spite of many errors on Steve's part. Problems included late shipment arrivals from Europe causing late deliveries to U.S. customers, communication problems with Johann, and cash flow deficits. In year three, Steve started receiving Internet and wholesale orders from Canada, Mexico, the Caribbean, and South America. What had started out as a simple part-time operation had grown to a small international business. Steve added other nautical product lines that complemented Johann's models. It was exciting, rewarding, frightening, and frantic, but compared to his old job of selling advertising, Steve loved it and he and Susan thrived beyond their expectations.

Closing Tip

Whether you start as a full-time or part-time business owner, always keep your mind open to new paths to follow. Just as Steve's story illustrated, many avenues will open as a business develops, and the entrepreneur needs to be open-minded and prepared to act on new opportunities.

PART II

Common Pitfalls—What Not To Do

The most common mistakes of aspiring entrepreneurs are pretty easy to identify. In this part of the book we are going to visit five entrepreneurs and witness the basic mistakes they made as they started their businesses. The characters that you will meet in these stories are real, as are the scenarios; only the names have been changed. Their mistakes are not made out of stupidity but caused by poor planning and inexperience. For the most part they fall prey to being so busy that they have overlooked some basic tenets that need to be followed to be successful. Often the best way to learn is from the mistakes of others.

You Mustn't Quit

When things go wrong, as they sometimes will
When the road you're trudging seems all uphill
When the funds are low and the debts are high
And you want to smile but you have to sigh
When care is pressing you down a bit
Rest! If you must—but never quit

Success is failure turned upside down
The silver tint of the clouds of doubt
And you never can tell how close you are
It may be near when it seems afar
So stick to the fight when you are hardest hit
It's when things seem worst that you shouldn't quit
—author unknown

6

Pitfall #1: Undercapitalization

D ONNA WAS EXCITED OVER THE PROSPECT OF MASS PRODUCING HER OWN line of designer T-shirts. It was a chance to combine her artistic skills with the retail knowledge gained over the past five years working in an upscale fashion boutique. With the encouragement from friends and family she had produced a limited test run of 500 shirts for distribution on a consignment basis through five local retail outlets. Using an effective, but limited, advertising program along with a professional point of purchase sign that directed customers to buy the newest look, they were snapped up immediately and the phone was ringing with requests for more stock and additional designs.

Her first decision was to expand from three to six designs and hire Bill, an experienced manufacturer's representative, to sell her shirts on his regular sales calls to women apparel retailers and at trade shows. They agreed on a 15 percent sales commission. Donna built a plan around a production run of 10,000 units as follows:

Retail price—$49
Wholesale price—$24
Cost of material—$8

Labor—$3
Overhead—$2
Sales commission (15% of wholesale)—$3.60
Net profit per unit sale (before taxes)—$7.40

Pretty good for starters, and if she could increase her future production runs to 20,000 units her net profit could increase to over $11 per unit. The initial objective was to run and sell the initial 10,000 units creating a $74,000 profit. That would be followed by another 10,000 run six months later, producing a pre-tax profit of over $100,000 in her first year. Using this projection she planned her estimate of initial capital needed.

Equipment, machinery—$10,000
Installation cost—$1,500
Material inventory—$80,000
Utility and rent deposits—$2,500
Legal, accounting fees—$1,500
Marketing materials—$2,500
Miscellaneous—$3,000
Total start-up cost—$101,000

Donna had saved $50,000 over the years, but the rest had to come in the form of a bank loan against the equity in her home. She borrowed the minimum needed, approximately $60,000, and went into production.

Bill took to the road and two major apparel fashion trade shows. The product was received with great enthusiasm and Bill easily sold the initial 10,000 units. Donna worked like crazy over the next three months to get the orders out. There were some unexpected problems and delays which caused some lost orders, but overall, commitments were met. The biggest obstacle was cash flow as Donna had failed to plan for late payment from vendors. Her initial capitalization planning only reserved one month's operating expense ($3,000). Since it took a month to get the first orders out and thirty-day trade credit was given to buyers, it was two months before any money started to arrive. In addition, 20 percent of the new accounts did not pay on time, many being 60–90 days late, and a few closed up and she received no revenue. Bill was upset as he had understood the commission would be paid on sales, not collections, creating a nagging problem that had to be solved. Donna was forced to return to the bank and request a short-term credit line until monies could be collected. The credit line was extended but the additional interest was another cash drain.

Although less than half of the $74,000 profit was realized, Donna got through it and made plans for her next season. That was when it hit home. Materials for the coming season had to be purchased. Suppliers were requesting $80,000 before revenues would be received, not to mention the operating expenses that had to be covered. The $40,000 remaining from her initial success was a drop in the bucket to what was needed. She had already mortgaged her home for $60,000 for the first run and now had no idea where to turn for the money to finance the second run.

Donna went back to the bank to request a larger loan against her home, but its value had fallen sharply during the past year and the bank could not rewrite the second mortgage. She was now very aware of her poor capitalization planning. Her business was off to a successful start, but it was very possible that she would have to forgo her dream unless a solution was found.

Long-Range Financial Planning

Donna was guilty of a very common error—planning for the startup but not looking down the road. It is not enough to just get the doors open. A new business owner needs to look down the road at least three years and prepare for the future. Donna had a very successful start to her business, but cash flow problems could shut her down even if profitable. With a longer-term view she would have anticipated that her financial needs in regard to purchasing materials would be greater. Armed with this foresight she should have requested a different arrangement with the bank. If properly explained and illustrated with a detailed cash flow analysis to the bank, she might have been granted a seasonal line of credit to accommodate her short-term needs for cost of inventory purchase. She may still get this, although the bank will be much more skeptical of her request in view of not being informed earlier. In addition, she should have consulted with her material provider to discuss extended terms of payment. Suppliers do not advertise this because they seek payment as soon as possible, but if the entrepreneur inquires he or she might be surprised at the accommodation that might be arranged depending on credit references. There are four pieces to a financial plan forecast: the initial start-up capital required, projected income statements to cover the first three years, the balance sheet, and the cash flow statement.

START-UP CAPITAL REQUIRED

Estimating how much capital is needed to open a business requires research and personal soul searching. This is not the time to be conservative as undoubtedly there will be surprise expenses. The following is a start-up cost estimate list for a typical retail enterprise:

Fixtures and equipment including cash registers—$25,000
Leasehold improvements (decorating, remodeling)—$18,000
Installation cost—$5,000
Starting inventory—$30,000
Deposits (utilities, rent)—$4,000
Legal and other fees, licenses—$1,500
Grand opening promotion/advertising—$4,500
Petty cash on hand—$500
Miscellaneous—$5,000
Total one-time-only expense—$93,500

This estimate is for all the costs that will be incurred to get the store doors open. However money will also be needed for the initial operating period until enough income is available to handle the everyday operating expenses. So in addition to the estimated start-up, one-time-only cost the entrepreneur must also estimate the monthly operating expenses. In this case the following projections are calculated.

Rent—$3,000
Supplies—$250
Utilities—$600
Insurance—$200
Salaries (not including owner)—$1,200
Advertising—$450
Accounting—$200
Loan payment—$600
Miscellaneous—$500
Total estimated monthly fixed expenses—$7,000

The total here represents only the fixed cost of operating the business, which may or may not include the owner's salary. These are expenses that must be met within the first thirty days of operation. A retail operation that collects cash on sales may be able to get away with just a one-month reserve. However, manufacturers and wholesalers who sell on terms or produce in advance, such as Donna, must put aside enough capital to carry the business until the bills are paid, often 60–90 days after the start of the business. New business owners should be able to devote themselves to marketing and operating the business in its opening process and not be tied down into trying to figure out how to pay the bills.

The two totals above represent the real capital needed to open the business. In this case $93,500 plus $7,000 ($100,500) is the capitalization amount needed to start this business. This may be in the form of cash, securities, loans, or investor money but it all must be accounted for in some manner before proceeding. Too many aspiring entrepreneurs try to circumvent the real truth and are in trouble starting day one.

The amount of money needed will vary greatly depending on idea and industry. As a rule there is a direct correlation between money invested and potential monies earned. A part-time hobby business may require a $5,000 investment and earn the entrepreneur $2,000, a 40 percent return on investment, which is very good if not too time- and labor-intensive. A full-fledged retail or wholesale business might require $50,000–$100,000 with a return of 15 percent after the owner pays himself or herself a reasonable salary. Manufacturing businesses may require more, depending on equipment. Franchise investment will depend on their track record and trade name and can be quite high but often have some financing assistance available from the franchisor. Many full-time business opportunities will require financing through a bank or loan institution or by inviting investors to join in the excitement. The financing part of the new business plan is the most difficult and it will often challenge the perseverance of the entrepreneur. However, if the desire is strong enough, and the plan is realistic, there will be a way to put a proper capitalization plan for a business together, although possibly the initial idea may be changed to fit the circumstance. A proper capitalization plan requires a well-supported, detailed plan of action, not just a guesstimate.

THE INCOME STATEMENT

The projected (pro forma) income statement, also called a profit and loss statement, forecasts the expected profit (or loss) from business activity over a designated period of time—usually a year. A business start-up should forecast a minimum of three years of anticipated profit or loss.

The statement shows the revenues, all monies received from sales or professional services, and all expenses and money paid out. It deducts the expenses from the revenues to show the net profit of the business over the period of time stated. The reason the new business should show this estimate for at least the first three years is to give evidence that it will evolve, if not initially, into a profitable venture worthy of loans or investor inquiries. If created realistically, it will also serve as a confidence builder for the entrepreneur. The following is a simplified projected income statement for the aforementioned retail business.

Sales, year one	$250,000
Cost of goods sold (includes freight charges)	$130,000
Gross profit (amount available to pay expenses)	**$120,000**
Less: Operating expenses	
Rent	$36,000
Payroll (not including owner)	$16,000
Maintenance	$1,200
Supplies	$3,000
Advertising	$5,400
Utilities	$7,200
Accounting/legal/license	$1,800
Interest on debt	$3,000
Insurance	$2,400
Payroll tax (employer social security contribution)	$950
Depreciation ($ allocated for equipment replacement)	$6,000
Miscellaneous	$6,000
Total operating expenses	**$88,950**
Projected net profit	**$31,050**

In this case, the retail entrepreneur is projecting a first-year net profit of $31,050. Since the business is a proprietorship, owners pay themselves from net profits. If there is debt, the note principal must be paid from net profits as well. The interest expense shown on the statement would indicate a loan of approximately $50,000 at 6 percent ($3,000 interest per year) which, if it is a five-year note, the principle would be $10,000 per year, leaving only $21,050 for owner salary or reinvestment. This might be satisfactory providing that years two and three of the projection show growth. A 15 percent sales growth in year two would add $37,500 to sales ($287,500) and approximately $18,000 to the gross profit. If the 15 percent growth rate is sustained through year three, the sales would rise to approximately $330,000, providing a gross profit of over $160,000. Providing the operating expenses grew at only 3 percent per year (approximately $95,000 at the end of year three), the net profit would equal approximately $65,000, indicating a potentially good opportunity. When the debt is paid off and sales grow this business should prove very worthwhile.

Years two and three can be shown in columns beside year one:

	Year 1	Year 2	Year 3
Sales	$25,000	$287,000	$330,000
Cost of goods sold	130,000	149,500	170,000
Gross profit	120,000	138,000	160,000
Less operating expenses	($88,950)	($92,000)	($95,000)
Net profit	$31,050	$46,000	$65,000

THE BALANCE SHEET

A little more complex, but just as important, is the business balance sheet. It is calculated very similar to the personal net worth statement shown in chapter 2. Its purpose is to show the worth, or value of the business, in terms of what it owns versus what it owes. A new business plan should show annual balance sheet projections indicating the growth of the business value over a period of three years. As in the projected income statement, its goal is to show that over this period of time the business will grow from its modest beginnings to a strong and profitable business entity. The figure below shows the opening day balance sheet for the above retail illustration.

The initial assets are taken from the capital needed statement. Current assets are assets that are considered reasonably liquid, assets that could be turned into cash within a twelve-month period. Fixed assets are assets that are more permanent and used to conduct business—building, land, equipment, and so on, and are more difficult to sell. The current liabilities are

Assets		Liabilities and Net Worth	
Cash (reserve + petty cash)	$7,500	Accounts payable	$0
Inventory	25,000	Current portion L/T debt	10,000
Total current assets	32,500	L/T debt	40,000
Fixed assets			
Furniture and equipment	25,000	**Total liabilities**	**$50,000**
Leasehold improvements	18,000		
Deposits	4,000	**Net Worth**	**23,500**
Total assets	**$73,500**	**Total liab and net worth**	**$73,500**

those debts that are due at the time of the statement and any portion of long-term debts that will be paid in the next twelve months. In this case it is presumed all start-up expenses have been paid in full and the only current liability is that portion of the long-term debt principal ($50,000) that will be paid within the next twelve months ($10,000). At the end of year one, the balance sheet should at the very least show a $10,000 improvement in regard to net worth since the first-year debt obligation will be met. If some of the monies from the net profit are also used to build inventory that asset will rise and the net worth will reflect that as well. This will hold true in years two and three which, if all goes as planned, will show a net worth considerably higher than the $23,500 shown on the initial balance sheet.

The projected initial balance sheet can show problems in regard to capitalization. Too much debt to equity will drown a new business. Banks often look for a 2:1 ratio of current assets to current liabilities. This assures them that if things do not go as planned there are enough liquid assets available to pay off debts. A risk-bearing entrepreneur may be able to move ahead with something less than 2:1 but should draw the line at a 1:1 ratio. More debt than assets can lead to unsolvable problems.

THE CASH FLOW STATEMENT

The cash flow statement is the most important of the three. It demonstrates what money is available, and when, to meet obligations. This was the problem with Donna's plan—she did not draw up a projected cash flow statement. If she had, she would have prepared herself for the cash needed to purchase materials for the upcoming season. Her projected income statement would show a healthy profit, but because her payment and receivables cycle are out of line, she is going to fail unless a solution can be found to assist her cash flow needs.

You run a cash flow plan on your household budget even if in your head. You know what is coming in each month and you know what bills you will need to pay. Some months the cash budget works fine and there may be a cash surplus. Other months such as December holidays or summer trips you may outspend your income. Without a plan to accommodate those months you end up behind in your credit card bills. A business cash cycle encounters the same problems.

The formula for following and projecting cash flow is actually quite simple.

Cash available at beginning of month
    plus
Revenues collected in month (note: collected may not equal sales)
    equals
Total cash available
    less
Expenses to be paid out (note: only expenses that will be paid, not owed)
    equals
end-of-month cash balance
    equals
next month's beginning cash balance

A business such as the retail store example above might look like this:

	January	February	March
Beginning cash	$7,500	$4,667	$6,789
Revenues collected	19,000	22,000	16,000
Total cash available	26,500	26,667	22,789
Expenses paid out			
Inventory purchases to pay	11,000	9,000	10,000
Fixed expenses to pay	7,000	7,000	7,000
Note principal	833	833	833
Owner's draw	3,000	3,000	3,000
Total paid out	21,833	19,833	19,833
Ending cash balance	$4,667	$6,789	$2,908

As you can see this will provide the owner with the foresight to plan on some dry months ahead with diminishing cash available. Based on this forecast she may wish to cut back on purchases or plan a reduction in salary, which she did in March. By laying this out in a twelve-month spreadsheet forecast it will show the good months and the bad months in regard to cash cycle. If there are months where there is a cash deficit the entrepreneur may have to discuss a short-term credit line with the bank to cover the deficits until surpluses appear, which quite often for a retail operation might be

October, November, and December. The bank will ask to see a cash flow projection to make sure the loan can be paid on a timely basis.

Table 6.1 shows a full twelve-month cash flow spreadsheet. By creating such a spreadsheet on Excel and monitoring it on a regular basis (usually weekly), the entrepreneur will escape the problems that Donna is facing with her designer T-shirt business.

Story Epilogue

Donna survived her mistake but not without considerable hassle and time delays which cost her customers. She returned to the bank with a begging cup in hand crying for help. The bank of course demanded to see a complete cash flow statement projection. Since the initial loan request was not adequate, they were dubious of Donna's planning ability and questioned many of her assumptions, which prolonged the decision. Eventually the bank arranged a six-month line of credit for $75,000, and if her projections proved accurate they would extend $50,000 of the $75,000 into the next selling season and then $25,000 of the $50,000 into the third season. By then her cash cycle should be stabilized. They also attached additional liens against her personal property and charged an interest rate well above the initial second mortgage granted. If Donna had created an accurate cash flow projection at the start she would have requested and received a larger second mortgage loan on her home and saved time, money, and lost customers. She was also encouraged to obtain at least a thirty-day trade credit from her vendors since she was now more established.

Closing Tip

Do not be overly optimistic in regard to planning your financial future. There will be unplanned expenses and miscalculations. In addition to laying out your hoped-for future, draw up a "just in case" plan for your personal reference. Make sure that if the latter comes true you can survive the initial months until you stabilize the operation.

Table 6.1

Twelve-Month Cash Flow Cycle

NAME OF BUSINESS		TYPE OF BUSINESS								DATE		
		Pre-start-up position		Month 1		Month 2		Month 3		TOTAL		
YEAR	MONTH									Columns 1–12		
		Estimate	Actual	Estimate	Actual	Estimate	Actual	Estimate	Actual	Estimate	Actual	
1. CASH ON HAND (Beginning of month)												1.
2. CASH RECEIPTS (a) Cash Sales												2. (a)
(b) Collections from Credit Accounts												(b)
(c) Loan or Other Cash Injection (Specify)												(c)
3. TOTAL CASH RECEIPTS (2a + 2b + 2c = 3)												3.
4. TOTAL CASH AVAILABLE (Before cash out) (1 + 3)												4.
5. CASH PAID OUT (a) Purchases (Merchandise)												5. (a)
(b) Purchases (Merchandise)												(b)
(c) Gross Wages (Excludes withdrawals)												(c)
(d) Payroll Expenses (Taxes, etc)												(d)
(e) Outside Services												(e)
(f) Repairs and Maintenance												(f)
(g) Advertising												(g)
(h) Car, Delivery, and Travel												(h)
(i) Accounting and Legal												(i)
(j) Rent												(j)
(k) Telephone												(k)
(l) Utilities												(l)
(m) Insurance												(m)
(n) Taxes (Real estate, etc.)												(n)
(o) Interest												(o)
(p) Other Expenses (Specify each)												(p)
												(q)
(q) Miscellaneous (Unspecified)												
(r) Subtotal												(r)
(s) Loan Principal Payment												(s)
(t) Capital Purchases (Specify)												(t)
(u) Other Start-Up Costs												(u)
(v) Reserve and/or Escrow (Specify)												(v)
(w) Owner's Withdrawal												(w)
6. TOTAL CASH PAID OUT (Total 5a through 5w)												6.
7. CASH POSITION (end of month) (4 minus 6)												7.
ESSENTIAL OPERATING DATA (non cash-flow information)												
A. Sales Volume (Dollars)												(A)
B. Accounts Receivable (End of month)												(B)
C. Bad Debt (End of month)												(C)
D. Inventory on Hand (End of month)												(D)
E. Accounts Payable (End of month)												(E)
F. Depreciation												(F)

Pitfall #2:
Missing the Target Market

G ERALD KNEW MEN'S FASHIONS AND HE KNEW THE FLORIDA MARKET, OR AT least he thought he did. He had been a manufacturer's rep for men's fashions successfully selling to South Florida retailers for over ten years. His customers were men's specialty stores, department stores, and golf pro shops.

It was a unique market. The colors were livelier and the styles more casual than any other part of the country with the possible exception of southern California. Salespeople from other parts of the country often chided him about the peculiarities of his market. Plaids, stripes, and paisley prints in pastel or shocking loud colors sold well in his accounts. If he sold a store dark colors or a conservative look, the merchandise would most likely sit for months before selling. The stylishly dressed men of the area wanted the tropical leisure or golf look. Gerald was successful because he knew what sold. He could sense the needs of the marketplace.

Starting to tire of the travel required for his rep job, Gerald took notice when a promising retail opportunity for a men's store opened up 200 miles up the coast in the area of Florida known as the Space Coast. It was located in a successful shopping mall in a town of 40,000 people. There was very little competition. Confident that his wholesaling experience and knowledge would lead him to success, he signed a lease to be the only men's store in the sixty-store mall. Gerald and his family were excited at the potential of the opportunity and made the move.

Purchasing the initial inventory for the 2,000-square-foot store was easy for Gerald. He traveled to the apparel mart to place his initial orders.

Casual slacks and shirts—$12,000
Dress slacks and shirts—$2,000
Sweaters—$3,000
Belts and accessories—$2,400
Sports coats—$9,000
Suits—$7,000
Ties, socks—$3,000
Total—$38,400

Approximately 80 percent of the casual wear carried the Florida look that he knew so well. There was some representation for the conservative dresser, but not enough to give a truly complete selection. The sports coats were splashy with prints and plaids and all the suits were in light tropical colors. Ties and sweaters were primarily of the same look and colors. The store décor also carried the Florida lifestyle look with mounted posters of Caribbean beaches and beautiful golf courses.

The store which opened with great fanfare proved to be a major disappointment. Instead of complements customers were overheard making snide comments about outlandish colors and designs. Gerald was shocked and confused as to the problem. After all, it was still Florida coastal living. As the customer count dropped, Gerald sought counsel with a local banker.

"Gerald, I've lived here all of my life. This community is unlike any other in Florida. Until the Kennedy Space Center arrived, we were basically a fishing community of 7,000 people. Now we are 7,000 people plus 15,000 engineers and their families. Engineers dress different from the Florida that you know. They go to work in dark dress slacks or skirts and short-sleeve dress shirts. Their golf outings are infrequent and there is not much in the way of long-term tourists as beach access is controlled by NASA and is often closed due to launches."

Gerald swallowed hard. He had made presumptions without research-ing his market. The target market was radically different from what was expected. He had a major problem on his hands which would not have hap-pened if he had done his homework.

The Importance of Target Marketing

Properly identifying the most lucrative market a small business serves can-not be overstated. You are not Walmart, Macys, or General Motors. You are a very small business with a very small marketing budget that cannot be wasted in trying to attract customers that will not come your way no matter what you are selling. The novice entrepreneur often falls prey to his or her ego. Having a strong ego and abundant self-confidence is a definite plus but it can get in your way if not careful.

Target marketing refers to breaking down the overall market for a product or service into manageable sectors that can be properly developed. Walmart is a mass merchandiser whose target market is comprised of practically the entire shopping community, although they concentrate their marketing efforts on those who strive for savings. The small business sector on the other hand thrives because it is more personal, unique, and knows its cus-tomers better. It cannot afford to conduct advertising campaigns on major television networks, metropolitan newspapers, or dominate Internet web advertising. It needs to concentrate on finding its own niche market and aim its marketing efforts directly at them through alternative, less expen-sive media. Not only does proper identification of the target market affect advertising choices, but it also directly impacts location decisions, product mix, price, and the appearance of the business.

Gerald learned the hard way. He missed the mark and ended up with the wrong product selection for the potential market. He might have correctly identified the demographics (age, education income level) of his customers, but he did not inquire as to the lifestyle (psychographics) of the market.

Although located on the Florida east coast, the engineering communities that make up the Space Coast have little in common with the upcoming professionals in South Florida who enjoy a social calendar and ample leisure time for the golf course. Nor would he be able to draw on a tourist market. If he had performed the necessary research and correctly identified his target market, he would have bought differently, advertised differently, priced his products differently and designed his approach, presentation, and location to accommodate the engineering community.

How to Determine Your Target Market

It starts by writing out a description of whom you see as your prime customer. For consumer goods this includes age, income, education level, sex, marital status, hobbies, and lifestyle. For business products or services it includes age of business, industry status, size, management team, product mix, location, and revenue generated. This consumer or business is the center of your target. Although you may be able to attract others who are outside of this description, the center of the target is your bread and butter. Figure 7.1 illustrates such a target:

Figure 7.1
Target Market Profile

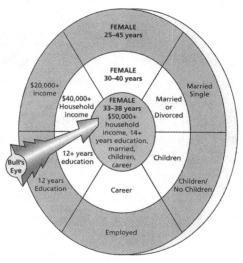

From Moorman/Halloran. Successful Business Planning for Entrepreneurs (with CD-ROM), 1E. ©2006 South-Western, a part of Cengage Learning, Inc. Reproduced by permission.

As illustrated, the customer profile in the target bull's-eye is identified as the market with the greatest need for your product or service. In the illustration the bull's-eye is very specific as to age, income, education, and career. It is not as simple as just women under forty. The outer rings show customers with similar profiles but who do not match the needs as well. These are rings that the business may grow into over the years, but it must first satisfy the inner ring if it is going to be successful.

Step number one is to make sure the target market in the marketplace is large enough to ensure success. If Gerald had written a description of his target market as similar to South Florida and then proceeded to do the necessary research as to its relevance to the Space Coast he would have changed his plan of action or looked for a different marketplace. It does not stop at just the demographic statistics but defines the lifestyle psychographics as well. Gerald was fine in regard to population and income but missed on lifestyle.

Table 7.1

Who Are Your Customers?

- Demographic study
  - Population
  - Age
  - Education
  - Income level
- Psychographic study
  - Describe the lifestyles
  - Where do they live
- Best customer profile
- Primary and secondary markets

Market Research

Very simply it requires research and often extensive research to support a new business idea. How large is the target market? What percentage of the market can your business reach? What is the competition and how strong is it? What industry sources of information are available? Can you justify a sales forecast? What is the market trend? What changes are occurring in the marketplace that may affect your future?

These are not easy questions, but the more information you collect, the less risk you will face. Let's walk through a real example of researching a market for a china and bridal registry gift shop.

Lina was a successful owner of a large gift shop. She was searching for a product that would help carry her through the slow summer season when she seized upon the idea of a china and bridal registry department. She had the space, 500 square feet, in the middle of her shop and believed she had the right clientele.

Her research started with a demographic study of the area. She discovered the following:

1. Her community was the largest of the seven communities in her county, and it was centrally located and growing. Total retail sales trends were on the upswing.
2. The average age of the county was in the mid-range compared to other counties in the state, as was education level.
3. Per capita income was slightly higher than the state average. Unemployment was pretty much in line with the state average.

There was nothing in the demographic study that would suggest it was not a good market.

Next she looked at the competition. Although there were some jewelers and florists that sold wedding merchandise, including special order china and invitations, she did not consider them direct competition for her target market of young newlyweds. There were two fashion department stores and a china shop in the next county some thirty miles away, but she considered them too far away to be of major concern.

Lina discussed her idea with representatives from the china and bridal industries. They agreed with Lina that her type of store in a market her size should do well selling their products.

Equipped with this information and her ten-plus years of successful retailing, she moved ahead with her plan. She created a beautiful boutique department that customers were most complementary about. Using her current operation as a guide in forecasting sales, Lina forecast first year sales of $75,000–$100,000 and bought inventory accordingly.

The results were not good; actual sales were less than $50,000. Since the rest of the store was performing to expectations, Lina was bewildered as to where she had gone wrong.

The answer to her question was she had not gone far enough in her research. She had made presumptions without support. Her contention that the jewelers and florists were not direct competition was incorrect as jewelers and florists are often the first stop for newlyweds so they have first contact with the bride and groom. The stores in the next county are very much competition as newlyweds-to-be will gladly travel to find what is best for their wedding. Did she properly filter the information from the company representatives by keeping in mind that it was to their advantage for her to open the new department? And lastly, but maybe the most important, her demographic study was flawed. She looked at the statistics, which was correct, but she also needed to look beyond the statistics. If she had she would have learned that although the population was growing, it was growing with retirees. The younger population was moving out as the older was moving in. She should have looked at the age trend, not just the raw number of average age. Also, if she had looked she could easily have discovered that the number of marriage licenses was declining over the past five years. With this cumulative knowledge Lina might have taken a different and more successful route.

Market Research Steps

There are six steps to performing a market research project.

> **Step 1: Define the question.** The question might be "who will be my best customer" or "how large is my target customer market?"
>
> **Step 2: Determine needed data.** What demographic data is needed, what primary (original) information is needed. .
>
> **Step 3: Collect the data.** A trip to the library and a search of the Internet is in order. Also determine what interviews, surveys, or opinion polls might help in gathering primary data.
>
> **Step 4: Analyze the data.** Study, compare, and question what you have to determine its value.
>
> **Step 5: Implement the data.** Using the data, make the decision yea or nay. Proceed with its creation or abandon it and move on to the next approach or idea.
>
> **Step 6: Evaluate the action.** Monitor and make adjustments.

Market research for a business is an ongoing process. The successful entrepreneur stays on top of the market and learns to anticipate changes and how to take advantage of them. Knowledge, determination, and creativity are necessary for success. Ask and research the following questions regarding the proposed market for your business.

- How big is the total market?
- How big is the target market?
- What share of the market can be attained?
- Who is the competition? What are their weaknesses? Strengths?
- Where is the location and why chosen?

The Marketing Mix

The marketing research allows you to prepare a plan for incorporating the proper utilization of the 4Ps of the marketing mix.

The right PRODUCT at
the right PLACE at
the right PRICE with
the right PROMOTION equals marketing success

By *product* we are referring to the total package of need satisfiers that your product or service provides. This is not limited to the tangible product. It includes the intangibles as well—the packaging, the guarantee, the service—all the components that lead to a fully satisfied customer. Knowing your target market on a personal level allows you to think through all of the needs they seek.

Place is the marketing tool that creates the perception that the product is easy to acquire. By knowing your target market you know where they go to find your product or service, thus you are able to choose a location that is convenient to them.

Price is an advantage, not a disadvantage, to a successful business. The idea is to make sure the price represents good value or exchange in the mind of the customer. Since you know your target market you will know what is acceptable and deemed a good value for your product.

Promotion is the way a business communicates with its market. Whether it is through advertising, personal selling, public relations, or promotional events the message must be sent to the right audience and clearly stated. Poor communication is expensive as it requires a constant resending of the same message. A small business cannot afford to ineffectively relay its messages to its customer base. Understanding the communication channel (see figure 7.2) is an important lesson.

The sender selects and encodes the words and symbols that will best express the communication, then proceeds to choose the best communication medium (print, verbal, e-mail, etc.); the receiver interprets or decodes the words, symbols, and so on as he or she understands or perceives them and then reacts by sending feedback or possibly no feedback. The feedback is how we determine the success of the communication.

The Xs in the figure represent the noise factors—all those things that get in the way of effective communication and can block or change the meaning of the message. This is similar to the game you played as a child of whispering

Figure 7.2
The Communication Channel

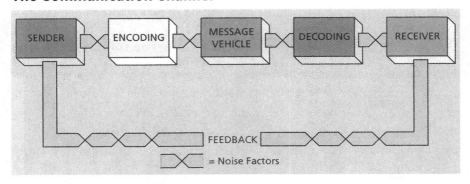

From Moorman/Halloran. Successful Business Planning for Entrepreneurs (with CD-ROM), 1E. ©2006 South-Western, a part of Cengage Learning, Inc. Reproduced by permission.

a message around a circle to see how it changed in its interpretation and translation. When you communicate with your customer base you want to eliminate the noise factors as much as possible. An ad that does not get through the noise factors has to be run many times, which is costly, and a promotion event that draws little attention is a waste of time and resources.

The essence of a small business is that we know the customers and their needs better than large businesses. We know their lifestyle, their budgets, and where they live. We can service them better, and that is the reason small businesses exist. Correctly identifying our target market allows us to communicate effectively, set our prices appropriately, and locate where our customers can easily and conveniently find us.

Expanding Your Target Market

As discussed, the initial target market is the exact bull's-eye of the target. As the business expands so may its target market. New product lines or services may be added, competition may fail, opportunities for expansion will arise. There may come a time to expand your marketing efforts to include the outer circles, but only after securing the bull's-eye group. You must concentrate on keeping your prime market while expanding to the outer market. Keep tabs on any changes that are occurring around your business. New competition, new technology that allows your business to reach new markets, such as e-commerce, competition that drops out, and economic cycles are ongoing happenings in all markets. Businesses are dependent on repeat customers. Learn to look at the lifetime value of customers, not just the immediate sale. A customer who spends $1,000 per year with your business may be worth $20,000 over the lifetime of the business. Do not risk $20,000 by determining that a $40 refund is unreasonable. The old saying that the customer is always right may not always be true, but it is the rule of customer satisfaction and long-term relationships. It is much more expensive to attract and gain a new customer than it is to retain a customer. Don't drop old customers; you never know when the needs that made them customers in the first place will return. Businesses that grow fast often forget the wisdom of retaining the initial small customers as they go after the big spenders. Go as far as you can to please the customer. You will lose some customers for reasons that you cannot control, but a good entrepreneur always has a plan to replace lost business.

When you decide to expand, rewrite your target market description. Make sure you are comfortable with the new target. Rethink the 4Ps to make sure they measure up to the expectations of the broader market. Do your research, conduct some surveys and, if all is right, expand your reach. You will need to determine strategies to attract new customers while at the same time retaining present customers.

Story Epilogue

Gerald was never able to recover from his mistake. Changing his product mix was helpful, but it took a full year to make the transition. The initial impression in the market was extremely negative and he was never able to gain their confidence. Competition entered the market in the form of a new department store with more conservative attire. The mistake in product mix led into the wrong price. The mall location was not the place for what looked more like a golf pro shop, and his efforts at promoting a more casual lifestyle in the engineering community fell on deaf ears. Within a year Gerald was back in South Florida successfully selling to the market he knew best.

Closing Tip

By answering the following ten questions, you will begin to learn about the psychographics of your customers. Knowing how they live will allow you to effectively design your market approach in a way that appeals to the customers' unsatisfied needs. Research the answers to the following target market questions.

1. What needs are being fulfilled by your product or service?
2. What segment of the market has the greatest amount of these unsatisfied needs?
3. How does this segment live that creates these needs?
4. How do these potential customers compensate if they are not able to fulfill their need for your product or service? Are there readily available substitutes?
5. Do they have the financial capability to purchase what you sell?
6. Who are the opinion leaders and trend-setters for your target group?
7. What common interests do the members of the market segment share?
8. What type of ambiance and environment appeals to their aesthetic sense?
9. What common values are shared by this group?
10. What common traditions are shared by this group?

Pitfall #3: Locating on the Wrong Side of the Street

EDNA HAD WANTED A COFFEE SHOP LOCATION ON POSH PARK AVENUE EVER since moving to the area five years ago. The tree-lined shopping area was four blocks of unique boutiques and eateries. Leading brand names and national merchandisers mixed well with local artisans and bistros. It was truly a dazzling collection to please the discriminating shopper. The area was so successful that rarely was there a store space available for lease. When one did open, the leasing agent would check a waiting list for interested tenants. Unfortunately Edna was not at the top of list, and there were several nationally known chain operations listed above her.

When a developer announced the acquisition of the old movie theater across the street from most of the stores with plans to convert it into a three-story shopping complex, Edna was one of the first to call.

There were to be eighteen retail spaces, each approximately 800 square feet. The tenant mix would be a collage of specialty retail product and food services. Each floor would have four retail shops, a small restaurant, and a specialty food server. The plan fit Edna's idea perfectly and she immediately signed a lease for a ground floor coffee shop.

In the nine months it took for the developer to finish out the project Edna learned the coffee shop business. She attended classes, worked with suppliers, and took a part-time job in a Starbucks. She created an outstanding look for her store and waited anxiously for the opening.

The Park Avenue Theater Shopping Galleria opened with great fanfare. With the exception of three spaces on the top floor, it was leased out and contained the desired balance of stores. The grand opening was a smash hit and the initial ten days surpassed expectations. There was some slowdown by the beginning of the second month as the curiosity factor subsided, but Edna was quite confident of her decision. However, at the end of month six there was genuine concern as the crowds were thinning and already two stores had vacated. Sales were very inconsistent and often very slow. Edna observed that the traffic on the other side of the street was quite good. What was happening?

The problem became apparent. As you see from figure 8.1 below, parking was primarily on the other side of the street behind the shops. To get to the Galleria customers would have to cross the street. Although the walk was only fifty feet and there was a crosswalk, customers still had to wait for a pedestrian walk light. It seemed like they were too lazy to make the effort and were quite content to shop the stores opposite the Galleria.

Figure 8.1
Park Avenue Shopping District Diagram

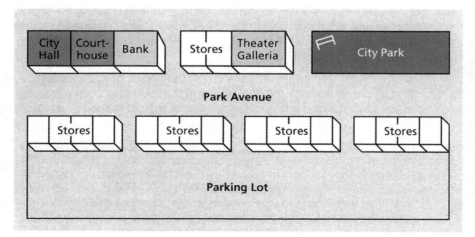

Location, Location, Location

I am sure you have heard the expression "location, location, location." It is important to you because it translates into convenience, convenience, convenience, which equals added profits to the entrepreneur.

The ever-improving efficiency of businesses in getting their goods to their customers has created a very spoiled society. Consumers and businesses have come to expect you to fill their needs with a minimum of delay, and if asked to wait or be inconvenienced they will say no thank you. Look what happened to Edna. Nice store and well managed, but crossing the street required time and effort to the customer and Edna did not fare well. The key word for both retail and industrial businesses is accessibility. The more accessible the business, the more sales and profits are generated. If you track the pizza industry over the past fifty years you see a significant growth rate. The reason: fifty years ago customers traveled to the local pizzeria, possibly across town, to get their pizza. Today pizza deliveries and multi-pickup or sit-down franchises make pizza a staple item in most households. We went from eating pizza once a month to, in many cases, numerous times a week because it became accessible.

Saving time is worth money to consumers and businesses and they are willing to buy more and pay more for it. Time is a commodity of value. Your neighborhood convenience store is the perfect example. Customers pay 20–30 percent more for convenience store products as opposed to giant supermarkets because it saves time. Entrepreneurs who can offer greater accessibility can make a larger markup and better serve their customers. Figure 8.2 illustrates what happens when a business is perceived as convenient.

Figure 8.2
Convenience Theory

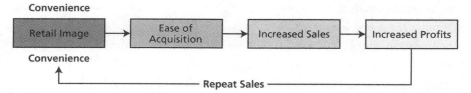

From Moorman/Halloran. Successful Business Planning for Entrepreneurs (with CD-ROM), *1E. ©2006 South-Western, a part of Cengage Learning, Inc. Reproduced by permission.*

Time and convenience have worked well for small businesses. E-commerce offers convenience in that there is no need to travel. Small manufacturers can compete with large businesses when they can be flexible and deliver goods faster.

Types of Consumer Goods

Consumer goods are often categorized according to accessibility to determine the optimum location.

Convenience goods are exactly what they say claim to be—convenient. They are goods that customers expect to find in many places. They can be found in convenience stores, drugstores, variety stores, and grocery stores. They require little effort or planning in their purchase. A business selling convenience goods must be very accessible because customers will not go far or comparison shop before purchase.

Convenience goods are usually sold in *neighborhood* shopping centers. These shopping centers usually consist of 4–20 businesses that serve the immediate neighborhoods that surround them. The tenant mix will be comprised of drugstores, convenience stores, dry cleaners, hair stylists, and other businesses selling primarily convenience products. Their lease arrangements are quite simple and less costly than the larger centers.

Shopping goods are not as easily found and usually stimulate comparison shopping. The products are normally available in sufficient quantities but customers will look for the best bargain or service before purchase. Shoes, tires, and popular fashions are examples of shopping goods. They require decision making much more than convenience goods and customers are more willing to expend some effort in their purchase. The location to sell these goods must be accessible and in most cases close to the competition to make shopping easier.

Shopping goods businesses are best suited for community shopping centers. *Community centers* are designed to serve the entire community in which they reside. Generally they consist of 20–60 stores and often have one or two anchor stores. Anchor stores are the well-known department store chains such as JC Penney, Macys, and so on, or big box stores such as Best Buy or Walmart that advertise heavily and have the ability to draw customers from all walks of life. These large stores bring the customers to the areas and the smaller businesses take advantage of their drawing power. By locating in these centers, businesses create an environment conducive to comparison shopping. The lease arrangements are much more complex, restrictive, and costly than the neighborhood centers, but if that is where your target market shops for your products, that's where your business must be regardless of the rent cost.

Specialty goods are products or services that are not as location-dependent because consumers are willing to extend considerable effort before making a purchase. These special products include wedding apparel, special occasion dress wear, cars, computers, and other products that require extensive research before purchase. Brides will travel great distances for a dress, computer geeks will spend much time researching for the right hardware, and prom dresses are not a casual pickup item. Therefore true specialty stores have more leeway in choosing a location, but they will have to make sure the customer knows of their existence through advertising and promotion.

Businesses that sell specialty products will be found in all types of shopping areas depending on their specialty. The nationally known specialty stores such as Crate and Barrel, Pottery Barn, and Victoria's Secret will often be found in *regional shopping centers*. These are the very large centers of more than 100 stores that because of the tenant mix and number have the ability to draw customers from several communities, often over 100 miles away. These centers are very costly and risky for the smaller businesses as they are primarily comprised of nationally known businesses with ample capital to operate in such an environment. If your specialty product is unique to your marketplace you may be able to do very well in smaller and less expensive shopping areas close to the larger shopping centers, with good exposure from the road and effective signage.

Some towns have vibrant downtown shopping districts which are often less expensive than the shopping centers but offer shorter hours. College towns and tourist destinations often provide good opportunities. They can be of particular interest to specialty good sellers.

Therefore the first challenge in determining the best location for a consumer product is to understand the importance of the convenience factor as it relates to their product or service. Edna's coffee shop competed with other stores selling specialty foods and beverages on the other side of the street. Customers evidently did not feel that her coffee, as compared to the competition across the street, warranted the extra effort required to cross the street.

Your location choice for consumer goods depends on your intended market and where your target market is most likely to shop. Make sure the demographics support the choice. You may wish to stay in your local community for your first venture if the demographics support the decision. You are more familiar with that market and probably have a network of banking and potential customers so you will not start from scratch. A new hair stylist should be able to count on friends and acquaintances to give her a try, which gives her a base to build on. Of course, if she burns their hair or applies the wrong hair color combination they will desert her quickly.

Don't Underestimate the Value of a Good Location

A common mistake made by new entrepreneurs is that they become too wrapped up in trying to save money on rent charges. As mentioned you must be where your customers expect to find you. If not, you will fail. The rent may seem high, but if choosing an alternative location costs you 30 percent of your customers you will regret the decision to rent a facility for a few hundred dollars less. The following example illustrates the difference a few extra dollars saved can mean to a business.

Two almost identical community shopping malls are located two miles apart on the same main thoroughfare of the town on the same side of the road. They each have space for fifty-five stores plus two anchor stores (see figure 8.3 below). Both centers have good occupancy with similar tenant mix. Shopping center A is anchored by a Sears and a well-known supermarket. Shopping center B is anchored by a JC Penney store and another department store. The rent for a 1,500-square-foot store (30' × 50') in shopping center A is $2,500 per month. The rent for the same size space in shopping center B is $3,500. This is quite a difference for what appears to be equal location, but beware. Shopping center A has a Sears, a very strong tenant, but when paired with a supermarket it has a definite flaw. Customers can easily park by the Sears to do their shopping and be on their way without walking through the rest of the shopping center. The same thing happens at the other end. Grocery shoppers cannot put their groceries in the car and go shopping; they need to go immediately home. Small stores in shopping centers are dependent on walk-by traffic created from customers' comparison shopping the anchor stores. In this case they lose that vital element. Shopping center B does offer that. When purchasing shoes the customer will check out both department stores for the best selection and bargains and along the way pass the storefronts of the other 53 stores. The owner of a card shop in both centers cites a 50 percent difference in sales volume between the two stores. That might translate into $150,000 versus $300,000. Saving $12,000 in rent is not a good decision if it means missing out on $150,000 in sales.

Figure 8.3

Competing shopping centers

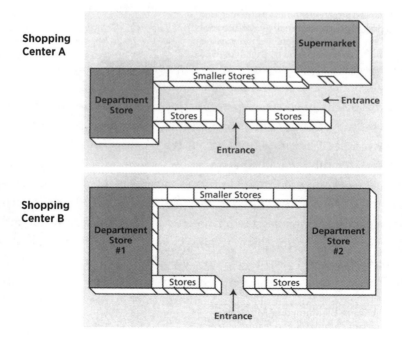

Locations for Manufacturers and Distributors

Manufacturers and wholesale distributors take different paths but they have the same goal in regard to location—customer accessibility. Accessibility to them means quick delivery time and physical and virtual communication contact. Shipping costs are a major expense to many of these businesses. Also, quick delivery of their supplies and materials is of prime importance to them and to their customers in order to meet their customers' needs. Being close to their delivery freight services and central to their customers saves time in transport. Moreover, since they will probably have a sales force that travels to their customers, the location decision will affect the sales cost of time and travel expenses. Many will locate close to metropolitan areas which host trade shows, thus allowing them easier access to these conventions.

Industrial parks. Most communities have industrial parks. These are sections of the community set aside for manufacturing and distribution businesses. Since numerous businesses are clustered together, delivery services are close by and very responsive to the needs of these important customers. Often the cost of land and buildings is partially subsidized by the city, county, and state in which they are located because they attract jobs to the communities and expand the community's tax base.

In recent years many communities have opened small business incubators for small manufacturers and distributors. The incubators are facilities that are owned by city or county business development agencies and rented out at very reduced charges with the hopes of luring new start-up businesses to their areas. They not only rent out the facilities but often include shared services for the tenants. There may be a common receptionist and reception space, meeting rooms, a library, and work break areas and vending machines. Often they are located in an abandoned factory in which each tenant has a partitioned-off section for their use. Incubators are also found near universities and receive their support from educational institutions. The only condition is that the tenants are only allowed to stay for a certain period of time, usually three years. At the end of the agreement the tenant moves into their own hopefully larger facility in the community. If all goes well by this time, the business has grown in terms of jobs created, income generated, and taxes paid. The community payback comes down the road as the employer continues to grow.

Start-up manufacturers and distributors should enquire to their Chamber of Commerce, banks, government economic agencies, and local universities and community colleges before determining a location. A tumultuous economy represents a very good market for these types of businesses in regard to location. States, counties, and communities are extremely interested in finding businesses that will increase employment in their locale and will work diligently to find the best situation for a new business.

Professional Office Space

Many professional services require an efficient-looking office space to meet with clients. Accountants, lawyers, real estate agents, counselors, and others must have a professional image and be conveniently located to be successful. Some businesses may look to the expensive tower office buildings in larger cities, while the majority of start-up small businesses will take a more practical look and start with a more modest but environment-compatible and accessible location to meet with clients. Many of the rules governing a retail location hold true for professional office location choice—it must be where your target market exists. As are retail locations, the rents are charged on a square footage basis, the cost depending on demand. There may be different arrangements ranging from fully furnished to just the room and space. There may also be shared common expenses with other office complex tenants similar to the incubators but not subsidized.

New to the market is temporary office space in which entrepreneurs may rent office space by the day or even by the hour. This is particularly helpful for businesses that work out of their home except when they need to meet clients. Airports often offer these arrangements for the traveling business person who can fly in, meet a client, and fly out without leaving the airport. This can be ideal for consultants. Needless to say, the hourly or daily rate is very high, but the offsetting flexibility without long-term commitment may make this type of arrangement very attractive to some professional business people. This is the day of the global entrepreneur who may meet with a client in New York and London on the same day. Airport office rental eliminates the travel time and logistics of getting from point A to point B in a city. They also offer services ranging from food and beverage to visual aid equipment

Home-Based Businesses

There are approximately 20,000,000 businesses in the United States that are operating from their home. Many are part-time. If a start-up business can operate from home by all means do it, because the advantages are many.

- Not only are there no lease, landlord, or rent costs but doing business from your home also has many tax advantages. You are able to deduct that portion of your home as a business expense. If you have a room dedicated as an office in a six-room house you are able to deduct 15 percent of your housing cost as a business cost. That goes for utility bills as well.
- The business is accessible to the owner around the clock. No travel to and fro, no traffic jams, parking hassles, or fuel costs.
- There are no lease restrictions or obligations imposed by lease rules.

Home offices are a great starting place for full- and part-time operations. Home-based businesses have blossomed with the growth of e-commerce. Internet selling through websites, eBay, and Facebook are three options that have caused the growth. All it takes is a computer, modem, telephone line, and the right product and you can start a business. Service-oriented businesses can do all their coordinating through their office computer. You may, once firmly established, outgrow your home. When you need more room for storage or additional staff or your client list has grown to the point where you need meeting space and display room, you will need additional square footage. Make sure your budget can take on the added cost of the lease before proceeding.

There are disadvantages as well.

- Do not use your home for a business if the business requires clients to come to the office. Having to walk through a crowded room cluttered with household items and a sleeping dog does not represent a professional image.
- Family activities can interfere with business matters. It is not easy to get the privacy needed to conduct business, particularly if there are children in the home demanding attention.
- It may get lonely. There is no water cooler or break room to chat with coworkers. Many will miss the social interaction. Some home-based business owners treat their day as if they are located in a downtown office by dressing appropriately and arranging regular lunch dates with colleagues and customers.
- A lack of discipline may lead to over-munching at the refrigerator or turning on the television to break boredom blues.

It will, of course, depend on your choice of business as to whether a home-based business can be considered. List the pros and cons, check with your accountant, and discuss with family members before deciding.

Leasing Versus Buying Considerations

If you are not operating from your home, you will either lease property or purchase a business location. Neither is a simple proposition.

Commercial leases are often long and very complex. Gone are the days of a simple handshake or one-page agreement. There is much to learn in regard to leasing terminology and obligations. The lessee (the tenant) may wish to consult a lawyer to make sure the agreement is what they believe it to be. Leases are a contractual agreement that state the lessee will pay X dollars to the landlord for a certain period of time. It does not say that if the business is no longer operating, the lessee does not have to pay. If you sign a three-year lease and call it quits after two years, you may still be obligated to pay rent for the final year. Lease agreements are like bank notes; they are for a stated amount of money to be paid in a stated period of time. Leases are written at the direction of the lessor and therefore protect the landlord.

Most commercial lease obligations are stated in terms of cost per square foot. The base rent for a 1,500 square foot space (30' × 50') might be $20 per square foot per year or $30,000 which is then divided into 12 equal payments, $2,500 per month. This is a base rent, but there may be other charges if located in a shopping center or large commercial office building. These might include:

- Common area maintenance charges. The cost of maintaining the property for such things as parking lot lighting or painting parking lines is borne by the tenants. Each tenant pays their share depending on the amount of space rented.
- HVAC charges are to cover the cost of air conditioning and heating of common areas. This might be for an enclosed shopping mall or an office building atrium. The tenant pays their share depending on the amount of space occupied.
- Tax escrow payments are collected from tenants to pay for the real estate taxes of the commercial complex. Again, they are proportioned by the amount of space leased.
- Insurance escrow payments are assessed to pay the tenants' portion of liability insurance to protect against injuries to anyone on common property. This is in addition to the business's own private insurance policy.
- Merchants association fees are common in community and regional shopping areas and are used to advertise and promote the shopping center as a whole. Each tenant pays their share.

These extra charges can add up, often 35–45 percent of the amount of base rent, so caution is the message. In addition a *percentage rent clause* may be inserted into the lease. A percentage rent clause requires the tenant to pay extra rent if their sales volume exceeds a certain percentage of their base rent. For example, a business agrees to pay 6 percent of their gross sales if that figure is higher than the guaranteed base rent of $2,500 per month or $30,000 per year. In this case if sales exceed $500,000 the tenant will pay 6 percent of sales as opposed to guaranteed $30,000 (6% of $500,000 = $30,000). If the business sells $600,000 in a given year the rent will rise to $36,000 as opposed to $30,000. The landlord feels the success is partly due to the conducive environment provided by the property while the tenant will believe it is due to their own hard work.

As stated, it becomes complex and if not confident, aspiring business owners need to consult with a lawyer. It should also be noted that leases are negotiable depending on demand and how much the property owner would like to add your type of business to their tenant mix. Don't be afraid to counter-offer a lease proposal. Lease expenses are tax deductible.

Buying a business location also has its pros and cons. In a good economy commercial property appreciates just like residential property, therefore your mortgage payments may be going to a good investment. All the negatives provided regarding leases are no longer a factor—you are the owner. You might also have extra space that can be leased out to increase your income and lessen your mortgage obligation. Although the principal paid on the property is not tax deductible all interest expenses are.

The down payment on commercial property is often higher and the mortgage payment terms shorter. If paying a down payment cuts into the amount of money needed for inventory or business operations, buying is not recommended. New business operations should ordinarily stay away from purchasing property until they are established. Once the business is secure and buying is an option, it should certainly be considered if the real estate market is on the upswing. If buying make sure that you thoroughly evaluate the facility. For some reason commercial property purchasers are not as picky as residential buyers although they face the same risk. Lessors should also thoroughly inspect the premises, but often they are better protected due to lessor obligations to provide a safe environment that meets all codes.

Whether you buy or lease a location the environment must be compatible with the business. Do not open a ladies fashion boutique next to a tire store or an art gallery next to a supermarket. Always keep the target market in mind—where will they be looking for you. Also make sure zoning ordinances are in your favor. Some communities have tighter control over business tenants than others. You may find that there are specific regulations that control signing, color, and other exterior appearance options.

Don't let competition eliminate a location. In many cases a business is better off going to where the competition is, particularly if it is strong competition. The strong competition has created a strong customer draw. By being close to that competitor your business can take advantage of the traffic that the established business has created. Remember, customers like to comparison shop and they will visit you as they are led to older business.

Apply research before determining where your business will reside.

Story Epilogue

Edna has survived but not without considerable pain. She realized that the only way to combat her secondary location was to create something very different and to take a very aggressive advertising and promotion approach. She became more than a coffee shop by adding a specialty cupcake product line. Cupcake stores are becoming a popular specialty food product, so Edna went back to the drawing board. She had to learn the cupcake business and buy the equipment. She met with suppliers and attended baking classes. Her investment was practically doubled and her operating expenses soared as she sponsored a semi-grand opening and greatly expanded her advertising. The result was that she created a business that was worth the effort to cross the street. Although she is still faced with the threat of the other stores failing in the Galleria, Edna feels her customer base is growing in loyalty and that if she must move in the future they will follow her if she is accessible. The lesson learned—don't assume your product is in itself enough to be successful. The "P" standing for Place is a most important ally in your quest to build a successful operation.

Closing Tip

Before determining a location go through the following steps and questions:

1. Can the business be successful in your home community where you have a starting base of customers?
2. Review carefully your target market—where do they expect you to be?
3. Where is your strongest competition located? If you sell shopping goods, investigate being close to them.
4. Do not go to a secondary location to save dollars on rent. There will be other ways to save money in the future that will not make you less accessible. Do not underestimate the importance of convenience and accessibility.
5. Ask around and get opinions from those shopping in areas you are considering. Look closely at how businesses in the vicinity are doing. Are there any trends?
6. What type of business was previously located there? Why did they leave?
7. Examine the potential facilities closely to make sure they are not in need of repair.
8. Review the lease or purchase document with an attorney.

Pitfall #4:
Inflexible Management

DON FELT MORE THAN CAPABLE OF TAKING ON THE SMALL AUTO PARTS DIS-tribution business he had purchased. After all, he had been a plant manager for a large corporation for eight years before deciding it was time to give small business owner-ship a try. He knew all about production scheduling, how to collect information, negotiating with vendors, and evaluating personnel. Don believed he was very well organized and knew how to run meetings. Although his sales experience was somewhat limited, he looked forward to attending trade shows and showing off his products.

Things did not start off well as he was confronted with the tremendous amount of duties required to keep his staff of ten employees producing at an acceptable rate. He would start each day by reviewing the incoming orders and posting them to the daily shipping schedule. The shipping sched-ule was written out in elaborate detail that would assure on-time deliv-ery. He used a plan he had developed in his previous job and had always proved successful. He used elaborate charts and spreadsheet printouts to explain the system to the workers. These tools required hourly updating and posting which took much of his time. The goal was to gain maximum output from each employee.

Unfortunately, the plan did not allow for absenteeism. Often one or more employees would call in sick on any given day, which would force Don to drop his other duties in order to fill in. This conflicted with his orderly plan and proved to be very frustrating to Don. In his previous job he had always been able to call the human resources department to send a replacement worker from another section to fill in for the absent employees.

Don was also frustrated with the incompetence of many of his workers. He was not used to the difficulty in trying to recruit skilled labor on a small company payroll budget which lacked many expected worker benefits. Consequently he was spending an inordinate amount of time training new workers and constantly reviewing procedures and processes with his staff. He was not able to find time to spend with customers, and sales were disappointing and headed in the wrong direction. The problems hit a critical point after six months when he was confronted in his office by six employees.

"Don, your scheduling plan is driving us crazy. We are doing our best but it never is good enough. You are so annoyed when you have to fill in that we are all uncomfortable and on edge. Your charts don't make sense so we ignore them. All of us here have worked in this shop for over ten years and until six months ago we enjoyed our work. Maybe we don't have the background of your previous workforce, but we give our all and care for this place. The new recycling plant is sending out advertisements for positions such as ours and some are very tempted to move over there if things here do not get better."

The timing of the meeting was not good. Don had just received their largest order of the year and expediency was of the essence. The pressures were mounting.

Five Functions of a Manager

No one told Don about flexibility. This is no longer corporate America with plenty of staff, trained personnel, and seemingly unlimited budgets. The five functions of management are planning, organizing, directing, staffing, and controlling. They carry into the small business world but in a greatly different application.

A number of years ago Dr. Rosabeth Moss Kanter of Harvard University wrote a book, *When Giants Learn to Dance*. Her primary message was to large companies stating that they were too rigid and they needed to take a lesson from small businesses in regard to flexibility. However, she also warned small businesses there was risk of a lack of discipline and regulation. The entrepreneur manager wears all types of hats and consequently he or she will not be as strong in some as in others. The guiding rule, though, is be flexible and creative but while staying on top of things.

Planning. All management starts with planning. All actions should follow planning. As an entrepreneur, your entrepreneurial life should start with a business plan (writing a business plan will be covered in chapter 11). Planning is laying the groundwork for goals and strategies to employ in operating the business. It covers all activities from budgeting to advertising. You start each year, month, week, and day with a plan. Learn to write out not only your daily plan but strategically look down the road a month, six months, a year, and even further. It should be evolving and never stagnant. Don't be afraid to change it as situations dictate. Large corporations cannot change direction quickly—too much bureaucracy—but a small business can change quickly and that is a strong point. Entrepreneurs cannot get bogged down; they must move fast when an opportunity arises.

For example, a small department store owner learned that a local bridal store was declaring bankruptcy. In a phone call to the owner of the bridal shop it was learned that a bankruptcy judge would decide in the morning how her property was to be liquidated. The department store owner had less than twenty-four hours to decide if she wanted to buy out the inventory at a very low price and create a bridal department. She also learned that another store owner was weighing the same proposition. In her future planning, she had recognized that her department store was lacking a summer stimulus, and one of her goals was to add something to make this happen, but she had not determined from where it might come. Everything she had learned in school and her previous corporate job told her "you cannot act that hastily." It takes time and research to make a decision such as this. Certainly large corporations do not act like this . . . so she bought it. Crazy, maybe, but guess what? It worked. The bridal business added a critical element to her business and gave her summer doldrums a great lift. The other potential buyer later admitted remorse but stated he was afraid to move on it in such a short time period. Did she violate a planning requirement? Not really. According to the buyer she spent the remainder of the day and early the next morning on the Internet gathering as much information about the bridal business as possible. Was it a complete research? Certainly not, but she wasn't totally reckless. Once the decision was made the buyer went into an intensive planning mode, laying out the department and forecasting its future after collecting sufficient information from sources she could trust.

Setting realistic goals is essential. Goals too easy to reach will not challenge while impossible goals will depress the workforce. Small businesses operate with a management-by-objectives guideline. Objectives for a particular period of time are set by the owner and the associates together. It is imperative that the employee is asked to participate as often he or she is in closer contact with customers than the boss. The objectives must be agreed upon, clearly understood, and written out. Periodically there should be times scheduled to meet to discuss progress towards the objectives. If progress is unsatisfactory these are the times to make corrections and adjustments. Determining that you are behind in your year-ending objectives in November does not allow enough time to correct the situation. At the end of the period final meetings are held to evaluate why or why not the objectives were achieved or missed. The results are then incorporated into the planning process for the next period of time.

A good small business manager needs to set aside time each day to think about the future. It is very easy to get so caught up in today's activities and decisions that we ignore the future. This is especially true when you are wearing the many hats of an entrepreneur.

Organizing. The organizing function of a manager requires assigning tasks. In a small business it is much more imperative to be able to delegate if the business is to move forward. As the business grows a single manager cannot do it all. One of Don's flaws was his inability to delegate. Those duties which assumed so much of his day could have been delegated to others, freeing him up to better fill in for absenteeism and contacting his customers. In addition, he would have been creating a more educated staff. There are no extra staff positions in a small business, so all must pitch in with fulfilling the mission. Small businesses are usually line organizations as opposed to line and staff organizations. In line organizations all employees are directly involved in the fundamental activity of the business. Line and staff organizations have both line positions and also staff or support positions such as accounting or a human resources department. Since line positions are employees that are directly involved with the goals of the organization they feel a greater belonging and loyalty to the business. Do not be afraid to delegate. It may take time to train and educate others for more responsibility, but in the long run it pays off. Even the smallest of businesses that employs workers should have an organization chart that shows positions and the responsibilities that go with the positions. (See figure 9.1.)

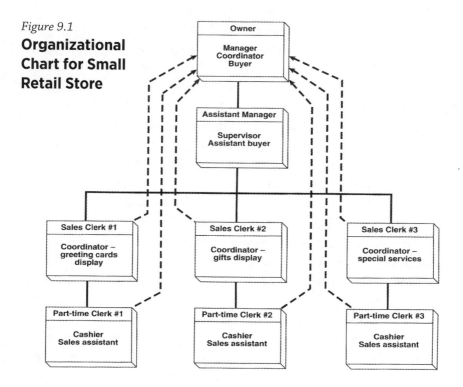

Figure 9.1

Organizational Chart for Small Retail Store

Directing. A good manager has a system developed for overseeing the operation and motivating others to accomplish the mission. This is directing. Just as a football coach inspires his team to win, a small business manager inspires his team to make sales and profits. Teams operate best when their leaders roll up their sleeves and dig right in with their associates. Don was a laggard in regard to this. The workers knew he did not want to be there beside them doing the everyday grunt work. If his attitude had been positive there would have been no such meeting. A good coach participates and also knows when to praise and when to discipline.

Staffing. Recruiting personnel into a small business is a challenge because, once again, the owner is faced with a limited budget. The big companies pay more and offer better benefits. They are able to recruit the cream of the crop, often leaving the leftovers for small businesses. This does not have to be if the entrepreneur creates the right environment. Referring again to Maslow's Hierarchy of Needs, the importance of meeting belonging, self-esteem, and self-actualization needs cannot be understated. An individual with very strong needs in these areas may be able to achieve them better in a small business under the right leadership. The staffing function must be coupled with effective delegation and training activities. The lower salary offered will often mean less experienced new employees. The entrepreneur must make up for the lack of skill with effective training and development. Small business training will be comprised almost solely of on-the-job training. It is certainly not as professional sounding as off-site education programs, retreats, or work simulation training, but in the long run it is the most thorough and cost-effective.

There are those who will sacrifice immediate financial gain for experience and opportunity if genuinely offered. A small business offers immediate involvement with many aspects of business operation. It can be a great starting place for the new graduate or an aspiring entrepreneur. There is selling to be done to these talented individuals, but a strong recruitment pitch of involvement, camaraderie, and future extra earnings when the business does well can be a powerful recruiting tool.

Controlling. Managers control their operations by staying on top of and monitoring what goes on. There must be control tools put in place that ensure quality, timeliness, and progress. Systems that control inventory levels, budgets, and operation capacity must be developed and maintained. There are numerous software programs available to today's managers. Quicken books, Excel spreadsheets, and scheduling layouts are examples. A major control tool that must be instituted is performance evaluations. All employees deserve to be evaluated and given an opportunity to improve and move up into higher salaried positions. Just as large companies have annual reviews, so should small businesses but on a less formal basis. The small business owner has, in many ways, created a family of associates and built a personal connection with them. It would be very awkward to announce to these associates that a formal meeting is to be held in two weeks for performance evaluation. It is more effective to invite them to lunch at a convenient time to review company progress. This would represent an opportunity to review where the employee fits into future plans and at the same time offer praise for past actions and suggestions for improvement for future assignments. When dealing with employees, build on strengths and not weaknesses.

Do not leave control of the finances to others. Many entrepreneurs become so dependent on their accountants they do not know their financial condition, which can lead to trouble. It is ultimately the business owner's responsibility, so he or she must be accountable, whether to the Internal Revenue Service or private investors. Small businesses are sometimes taken advantage of by unethical bookkeeping services. Embezzlement by such services or sometimes employees is all too common and is a result of poor owner control regarding the business's most important asset.

Leader vs. Manager

A manager is not necessarily a leader. A manager manages—stays on top of things, plans, organizes, directs, and controls. A leader inspires, creates a vision, and steps forward. If the entrepreneur has employees, he or she will need to lead as well as manage. So what makes a good leader?

Participative leadership. Leaders back up what they say by doing it. They listen. They are democratic, not autocratic. A store owner should find time each day to work the cash register no matter how large the operation. The manufacturer should spend time each day working on the floor with the workers. The service provider should pick up the telephone. There is no ivory tower in the small business world. Executive hierarchy and privileges are left behind in the corporate world. Managers are equals with their associates. They go to lunch with them, attend their baby showers, and participate in birthday celebrations.

Theory Y leadership. Eighty years ago management theorist Douglas MacGregor categorized managers as Theory X or Theory Y. Theory X managers are production-driven at the cost of personal relationships. Getting the job done is more important than how it is done. Theory X managers take a drill sergeant approach to the workers. They do not believe workers like their work and wish to escape responsibilities and challenges. Theory Y managers are the opposite. They believe cooperation and mutual dependence are essential to quality work. They believe their associates enjoy their work and want challenge and responsibility. A small business owner/manager who is also a leader will practice Theory Y management style while at the same time recognizing the need for a Theory X approach during times of crisis. Theory X mangers can get results through fear tactics but it will not be long lasting. Often large businesses will take the Theory X approach in quick turnaround situations, but to be effective in the long term Theory Y is much more conducive to reaching goals. The small business leader does not need fear tactics to gain desired results. He or she should be charismatic and transformational in that they gain trust from associates at the same time they make things happen. It is only on very rare occasions that they will use the authority that accompanies Theory X behavior and when they do it is appropriately administered.

Hygiene versus motivation factors. About the same time MacGregor was floating his Theory Y versus Theory X principles, a fellow named Herzberg was citing business owners and managers for not going far enough. Surveys would indicate that most employers would proudly tout that they paid a fair wage, provided good supervision and policies, and allowed a friendly social environment. Herzberg's study determined that was not enough; they were only doing what was expected, and Herzberg labeled these basic offerings as hygiene work factors. If they truly wanted workers to perform at their maximum productivity, the employers needed to offer challenging and personally satisfying opportunities. Workers respond greatest when given responsibility and autonomy. You as a small business owner need to keep this in mind right from the start. A first-day employee should go home after the first day and proudly announce to friends and family what he or she accomplished that day. A retailer should allow a first-day employee to set up a display or give input into an advertisement. A manufacturer might ask a new employee to review the specs of a job with a customer. These types of acts will have the effect of giving an immediate feeling of belonging and self-actualization.

Leaders are visionaries who can excite. They not only see clearly the objectives but also communicate the visions and rewards. They are charismatic and transformational. They understand motivation and know how to reward and discipline in a manner that is effective. They do not flout their authority; it is not necessary. People will respond to them out of respect and confidence in their decision making. A small business owner with employees should be both a manager and a leader. There is no buck passing. The owner is the captain of the ship and has full responsibility for the organization. It is not possible to successfully guide the business by yourself. You will need the help and support of those who are part of the business. There are many books on managing and leading; entrepreneurs need to educate themselves and learn to employ the leadership style that suits their type of business.

The Effective Small Business Leader

In his book, *The 7 Habits of Highly Effective People,* Stephen Covey lays out a path to success for an entrepreneur to follow in building a successful enterprise. An enterprise will be successful if it has the right people supported by the right leader. Covey points out seven habits that can get you there if you take the time to develop them. In many cases he points out there needs to be a definite paradigm or shift of the way we are used to thinking. It takes time and practice to change from our old ways of thinking to new ways. Ask any golfer who has tried to change his or her swing or an ex-smoker how hard it is to break the habit. Our mindsets are habitual. If you think pessimistically it becomes a habit and affects the way you look at life. If you are a control freak, it is hard to delegate. Narrow-minded people need to relearn how to view the world objectively. All of this takes effort and the realization that you can do some things differently and improve your leadership abilities.

Covey's seven habits are designed to move individuals from dependence in which they look for others to take care of them to independence in which they believe they can do it all themselves to a third stage of interdependence in which they recognize that they will be successful only by working together with others.

Habit 1: Be Proactive. Don't wait until the event happens to take action. You are responsible for your own actions and decisions. Do not blame circumstances. Reactive people wait for the other shoe to fall, they allow their environment to dictate their decisions. If the weather is poor it affects their attitude. They are driven by circumstance. By contrast, proactive people are driven by values. Covey suggests taking a day to listen to yourself and those around you. How often do you hear "if only" or " I can't"? If you catch yourself using these types of phrases you need to move away from being reactive to being proactive.

Habit 2: Begin with the End in Mind. This requires writing a personal mission statement. A personal mission statement should state who you are, where you are, and where you want to end up. We will discuss your business mission statement in chapter 11, but it will closely align with your personal mission statement because the business is really an extension of you. Keep an eye on the end and don't let circumstances lead you astray.

Habit 3: Put First Things First. Habit three is the actualization of habits 1 and 2. It is all about practicing effective self-management. It takes discipline. It is creating the ability to say "no." It means learning to determine what is urgent or not urgent, what is important versus not important. Building this habit allows you not to waste time on things previously believed to be essential when they were truly not. Small business owners should become masters at this since there is no time to be wasted in building a successful business. By putting habits 1 and 2 into place with this habit the individual should arrive at the stage of independence. While this is certainly an important step up from dependence, there is still a way to go.

Habit 4: Think Win/Win. Covey points out that there are six paradigms of interaction.

1. **Win/Lose:** If I win, you lose. Very authoritative and power-driven. Very competitive and built on a low trust attitude which should not be a small business owner's philosophy.
2. **Lose/Win:** This "I lose, you win" is an appeasement approach which is certainly not characteristic of a leader. Always trying to please to achieve popularity is not value-based and does not work in any business environment.
3. **Lose/Lose:** When two win/win people collide the outcome will likely be they will both lose. To make matters worse, they may become vindictive. There is no compromise; they would rather lose than compromise.
4. **Win:** This is the "if you don't play my way I will take my bat and ball and go home" philosophy. All that matters is that they get what they want, no matter the consequences. In other words, I will not refund a purchase no matter if I lose a lifetime customer.
5. **Win/Win:** In a win/win situation all parties benefit. It is the cooperative way. No one gets hurt. This is certainly the path for success.
6. Covey then adds an addition to win/win and calls it **win/win or no deal.** Very simply, if the parties cannot find an answer that benefits all, they just don't make a deal. It is "I only want to win if you win also." Sounds a bit utopian, but in many small businesses we find that kind of an arrangement. Why not deal with vendors or customers with that understanding? Don't buy from a supplier who, although they profit from your purchase, do not appreciate the correlation of your long-term success to their success. You in turn must feel a desire to build on this relationship for the long term.

Habit 5: Seek First to Understand, Then to Be Understood. In other words, learn to listen. Often we do not listen to understand, we listen to reply. We are concentrating on our reply more than we are intent on listening to what the speaker is trying to get across. Listen with empathy, not anticipation.

Small business owners will learn so much about their customers and how to sell to them by mastering listening skills.

Habit 6: Synergize. When we synergize we are creating a whole that is greater than the sum of its parts. We develop a conceptual skill that allows us to see how all the parts come together to produce the final offering. Synergizing recognizes new possibilities and options. It opens the mind by breaking down mindsets. Being open with high levels of trust will produce solutions better than thought possible. It adds to a creative enterprise. It communicates cooperation and trust among all involved. It is the final step to interdependence.

Habit 7: Sharpen the Sword. This is Covey's way of telling us that to be effective we must continuously practice and renew these habits. These habits enhance us and bring together the physical, spiritual, mental, and social/emotional dimensions of our character.

Story Epilogue

Don was faced with an enormous dilemma. A big order needed to go out and the workforce was angry and defiant. He felt he was being held hostage or the order would not go out. Don relented to the workers by apologizing and promising to get rid of the inflexible scheduling routine and working more cooperatively with them in the future. The order went out but Don failed dismally at his promises. Within two months four workers left for the recycling plant operation and Don did not have enough trained workers to successfully serve his clients. Nine months after he had bought the business, Don sold out at quite a loss and returned to the corporate world where he belonged.

Don is certainly not alone as an individual who struggles to change the habits and attitudes ingrained after many years of working in large businesses. He really needed to heed the advice of Steven Covey and others on how to treat employees and be flexible in their approach to managing others.

Closing Tip

In making the transition from working for others to being the head guy in a small business, make sure you are prepared for the change. Read management books, attend seminars, and talk to others regarding their experiences. It is not an easy transition and some cannot make the change because it requires, in the words of Stephen Covey, a dynamic paradigm shift in habits.

Pitfall #5: Trying to Compete with the Big Boys on Price

R ON WAS FRUSTRATED AS HE SAT IN HIS STOREROOM OFFICE STUDYING HIS sales reports. His audio sound store business was struggling due to the new national big box discount store that had entered his marketplace last year. Having finally achieved a profit after four years of hard work, his future was suddenly looking dim. Sales were dipping and the profits disappearing. He wondered if he should try beating the discounter at their game—lowest price. Their prices were averaging 15–20 percent lower than his. He wondered how many more units he would have to sell at a 20 percent discount to increase his profits. He started by looking at last year's income statement and based on results from "on sale" merchandise he factored in that a 20 percent retail price discount would give him at least a 25 percent increase in units sold.

Previous year		Projected with a 20% discount	
Sales (5,000 units at $100 avg. transaction) =	$500,000	(6,250 units at $80) =	$500,000
Cost of goods (5,000 units at $52) =	$260,000	(6,250 units at $52) =	$325,000
Gross profit	$240,000		$175,000
Operating expenses	$180,000		$198,000
Net operating profit (loss)	$60,000		($23,000)

Wow! Ron realized this was not good. To discount you either needed a much better purchase arrangement or a bigger increase in unit sales than he thought. In discussing the idea with his vendors he learned that buying an extra 25 percent in units would not enable a larger unit discount for a small business such as his, and he knew that selling more units would drive up his operating cost. He took another look and adding in additional advertising, factoring in a 50 percent increase in units sold if sold at a 20 percent discount. He also inserted a 10 percent vendor quantity purchase discount at this volume.

Sales (7,500 units at $80 avg. transaction)	$600,000
Cost of goods (7,500 units at $47)	$352,500
Gross profit	$247,500
Operating expenses	$210,000
Net operating profit	$ 37,500

Profit, yes, but still below his previous position. And this did not account for the additional space he would need to store the extra inventory. This is absolutely crazy, thought Ron. I wonder at what level it makes sense? A 100 percent increase?

Sales (10,000 units at $80)	$800,000
Cost of goods (10,000 units at $47)	$470,000
Gross profit	$330,000
Operating expenses	$230,000
Net operating profit	$100,000

Finally, an increased profit, but at what investment and risk? To sell 10,000 units he would have to rent larger space, spend significant amounts of money on promotions, and increase storage space to store the additional inventory. If he borrowed money to purchase the increased inventory there would be additional interest charges, not to mention insurance. All of these expenses would be in addition to the increased payroll and supplies he had calculated into his planning.

There must be a better way.

The Role of Price

Price is included in the 4 Ps because it should be a marketing tool, not an inhibitor. The price of a product should be communicating that this is a good value for the exchange. In a small business price includes the value the small business owner brings to the customer in regard to quality and caring. The pride of small business is that they do things better than the large businesses. Small businesses are flexible and caring—they go the extra mile. If this is true, why do so many decide to take on the big boys in terms of cost leadership? Since they deliver more value, they deserve more, not less. And as a matter of fact, they need a larger profit margin if they are to be successful. Large corporations that are making a profit of 2–3 percent of sales are considered successful. In most small businesses, the owner may need to produce a profit of 10–20 percent of sales to be successful. A simple breakdown on a $100 sale might look similar to:

	Retail store	Service provider	Manufacturer
Income	$100	$100	$100
Cost of goods/materials	52	30	24
Gross profit	48	70	76
Operating expense	35	55	66
Net operating profit	$ 13	$ 15	$ 10

From this profit the owners must compensate themselves, pay back any debt, pay taxes, and reinvest money to keep the business growing. Using the example above, a small business with revenues of $500,000 would be producing a profit of between $50,000 and $75,000, which does not leave much wiggle room for error.

This is why it is so important to protect the profit margin. A small business that discounts is in all reality only discounting from the owner's profit as most expense percentages are quite fixed. Therefore when you reduce the $100 revenue to $80 most of that reduction comes directly from the profit. An independent retail store offering a storewide sale of 20 percent off will in all likelihood not be open a year later. This is not the suggested route for the small business. Protect the margin and add to it by providing special perks which add to the product value. A large business cannot do this as well as you can.

The price of the product or service must accomplish the following:

1. Cover the cost of the item to be sold. This would include not only what is paid to the supplier but also the cost of any shipping or delivery charges.
2. Represent a good value to the buyer.
3. Cover all operating costs associated with the exchange (rent, payroll, supplies, etc).
4. Provide a fair compensation to the owner for risk and effort contributed.
5. Make a contribution to the long-term stability and growth of the enterprise. There needs to be enough retained earnings for reinvestment in increased inventory, remodeling, and so on.

Most small businesses are quick to identify the necessity of the first four but are guilty of ignoring the necessity of number 5. A business that fails to grow will eventually fail.

Determining Price

Setting your prices can be a complicated process. Arriving at the right price will depend on your choice of strategy and a basic understanding of supply and demand principles. As you may recall from your study of economics, consumers can buy what they can afford, so the higher the price for a product or service the smaller the market. As price rises, demand falls. As prices fall, demand grows. If there is a surplus of similar goods in the marketplace, prices will fall in order to sell the surplus. If demand is high for a product and the quantity is limited, the sellers of the product can sell at a higher price. So the first question is how limited is the quantity of your good or service in your marketplace and how many competitors are trying to reach your target market.

You will need to determine the amount of products or services to be sold to make sure that all costs are covered. You can derive an estimate by conducting a break-even analysis. This requires adding up your estimated fixed costs (costs that do not substantially change regardless of sales activity). Examples of fixed cost for most businesses include rent, utilities, insurance, and other constant costs of operations. You must cover these costs with the profit margin from your sales. If you determine the annual fixed cost of operation is $100,000 per year, you must price your product high enough to cover that amount plus the cost of the product, which is a variable cost because the amount you pay for the cost for goods depends on how many units you expect to sell. There is a formula. (See also figure 10.1.)

Break-even point = Fixed costs ÷ Contributing margin

If your estimated fixed cost is $100,000 per year and your average unit transaction profit margin (contributing margin) is $25 ($50 retail sale less $25 cost), the break-even point (BEP) would be 4,000 average transactions.

$100,000 (fixed cost) ÷ $25 = 4,000 units, BEP

Figure 10.1
Break-even chart

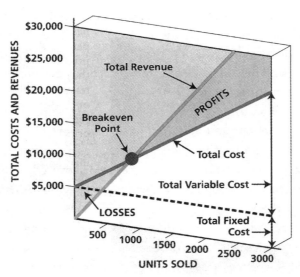

Pricing Strategies

The new business has a variety of choices in determining their initial pricing strategy. In the long run the customer will determine the business's overall pricing strategy, but in the beginning stages there will be various options available.

The first decision is to determine if you are to take a cost leadership or a differentiation position in your approach to the marketplace. Are you offering a price advantage to your customer or a unique product or shopping experience? As indicated, most small businesses achieve success by offering a more unique and personal experience to their customer as opposed to trying to compete strictly on price. Often this leads to creating a niche market position or one that is highly focused on a very specific target market such as the ship in a bottle seller mentioned earlier in the book. This choice will determine your final pricing position as either low price or higher price depending on the uniqueness and supply and demand of your product or service. Pricing strategies vary significantly. In cases, particularly in the service industries, price may be an inhibitor until word of mouth spreads to enhance your professional reputation. A plumber who moved from New York City to Atlanta posted his prices quite a bit higher than the local competition. Many told him he could not get away with New York prices in Atlanta but he confidently stuck to his prices because he believed his service was superior and he should be paid more. It took time but he was eventually proven correct and his business now flourishes despite his higher prices. Consumers will pay more for unique products and superior service

Market penetration strategy. Often used as a short-term pricing strategy, market penetration is selling at the lowest possible price to attract initial market share. A new business needs to be discovered before it can grow and one method is through announcing great savings. This allows gaining customers at the expense of your competitors. This strategy can work but should be used only as an introduction for a new business or product line. Eventually the price will have to rise to a profitable level after customers have gotten to know the business for more than just cost savings. It is important when implementing this strategy that the small business announce that it is a temporary savings. "Grand Opening Specials" or "Introducing Our

New Department" are examples of using a temporary market penetration strategy.

Skimming is the opposite of market penetration strategy. Skimming is asking for the highest price possible for a new product or service. It works particularly well in new technology products that are only available in certain outlets. The seller is aware that there will soon be competition entering the market but will want to make the most from their unique product offering while they can. When Texas Instruments introduced the first electronic pocket calculator it was priced at a $175 retail price and sold well. Competition entered quickly, forcing the price down and now many years later they sell for as little as $5.

Loss leading. Businesses actually do sometimes sell products at an intentional loss. This is done on the idea that customers will come to the business to buy the loss-leading product but at the same time will buy enough of the full-priced other products to make up for the loss. You see this often at supermarkets and drugstores; for example, a gallon of milk or a case of soft drinks are priced at very low prices to entice but the business is also counting on the customer to buy their remaining food or drugstore needs while in the store. They sacrifice a dollar on the milk in order to sell $100 of additional groceries. Manufacturers and distributors might also use this strategy at trade shows in order to sell their other products at profitable prices. It is a strategy better suited for big businesses with a very large selection of convenience goods.

Price lining. Some businesses will group items together under one price, such as all items on this display are $10. It makes customer decision making simpler. The idea behind price lining is to mix the items sold slightly under $10 with items usually sold over $10 to achieve the desired profit margin. It can be risky as the items intended to sell higher might outsell the lower priced goods, causing the ratio to be out of line with the desired profits.

Price bundling. This is a pricing strategy that is aimed at making multiple sales. "Two for the price of one" or "buy three tires and the fourth is free" are examples of price bundling. It is sometimes useful as a market penetration strategy or a way of reducing surplus inventory.

Status quo pricing. Once the dust settles and the business has gained market share it will most likely set price levels at a relatively fixed level. This status quo pricing strategy maintains prices in a certain range unless there is a change in the marketplace such as new competition or a bad economic cycle. During times of such developments the entrepreneur must be open to consider at least a temporary change of pricing strategy in order to better compete for customers. He or she might revert to a market penetration strategy to prevent losing customers until the crisis has eased.

Price point psychology. It is important that the business owner understand the psychology of price points when setting a price. $9.95 compared to $10 does make a difference to many customers. The $9.95 means less than $10, just as an automobile priced at $29,990 means less than $30,000. How often has this impacted your purchasing decision? Haven't you been guilty of telling a friend that you paid less than $100 when you paid $99? Price point psychology can work to the advantage of the business owner. There is very little difference between $89 and $99 as neither passes the objectionable $100 price inhibitor. Consequently this allows the business to consider selling an $89 product for $99, but also keep in mind that a product that should be normally priced at $110 may be better marked at $99.

THREE STEPS TO DETERMINE PRICE

Step one: Survey the competition and determine if a surplus or shortage exists for your product or service. Keep a vigil on your competition by visiting their stores or websites. Also watch their advertisements. If they are putting products on sale it is possibly due to either a surplus inventory or a cash shortage.

Step two: Do an estimated break-even analysis to make sure that reaching a break-even point is easily attainable. Use the formula cited or calculate using your projected sales and cost figures to discover at what point you will cover all your operating and inventory purchase cost. Once the break-even point is reached the fun begins because each succeeding unit sold brings increasing added profits.

Step three: Determine your pricing strategy, keeping value exchange in mind. Remember, price should create a positive feedback in relation to the satisfaction that will be achieved through purchase.

The greatest detriment to making a sale is price. Customers must believe the value of exchange is fair. Often called the hidden objection, salespeople must understand how to react to this hidden inhibitor. It may be disguised as "I don't like the color" or "It is too large" when it is really "I don't like the price." Good salespeople know how to identify this and usually answer the objection with a question. Once a price objection is determined, questions like "If you wish, we can arrange a payment schedule?" or "Did you know we have a layaway plan?" are asked. It is an example of adding value to the exchange.

Markup and Markdown

Determining markup and markdown percentage will vary depending on industry. Markup is the difference between the original cost of the product and the requested selling price. It can be expressed in dollars or as a percentage. If an item that costs $50 is priced at $100, the markup is $50 or 50 percent of the retail price.

When you know the cost of the product and want to receive a 60 percent markup, you can divide the cost by the reciprocal of the desired percentage; for example, a $60 cost with a 40 percent markup = $60 / .60 = $100 selling price.

If you know the retail price and want to know the cost and you know the markup percentage, multiply the retail price by the markup and subtract the answer from the retail price. If the retail is $100 and the markup is 50 percent, $100 × .50 = $50, $100 minus $50 equals the $50 cost of the product.

When you know the cost and retail and need to know the markup percentage, subtract the cost from the retail price and divide the difference by the retail price. The cost is $50 and the retail is $100. To find the markup, subtract $50 from $100. Divide the difference of $50 by the retail price of $100 and the answer is 50 percent markup.

As mentioned, the desired markup varies by industry but the same formula applies. The grocery industry may exist with a 20 percent markup of retail price while a manufacturer may need to sell at a 400 percent markup of cost of materials to cover all fixed and variable costs.

Markdowns are a necessary part of pricing. Not all goods will sell at the original asking price. There will be many reasons to discount the original price of the product: to hold special promotions, sell obsolete products, address seasonal fluctuations, or divest oneself of damaged goods. The amount of markdown will depend on the immediacy of the situation. The rule is to take them as soon as possible. Your goal is to redeem the products for cash in order to reinvest in newer or next season products.

Remember, price is largely determined by competition and what the market will bear. Experience is the best teacher.

External and Internal Variables That Affect Price

Earlier in the chapter we mentioned that new competitors and what the existing competition does will affect how you price your products or services, but there are other factors that create chaos. One external factor is economic cycles. The marketplace certainly did an abrupt turnaround starting in 2008, particularly in the housing and construction markets. Changes on the economic environment can encourage or discourage consumer buying. It is easy to get tricked into thinking that what happens in Washington doesn't affect a business in Paducah, Kentucky, but eventually it will. A recession will cause people to stop spending and save, inflation may cause panic buying or serve as a price inhibitor, and a drop in interest rates or a tax rebate will provide more cash to consumers, which ordinarily creates spending. Entrepreneurs must keep an eye on the economy and be prepared to change direction if the economic cycle changes dramatically.

Societal changes are another external variable that can change spending habits. Changing ethnic patterns, attitudes, and laws can affect people's lifestyles and spending habits.

Technological developments may bring new products to the marketplace and may make other products obsolete. The entrepreneur may have to change markets if the entrepreneur's product becomes obsolete in order to stay up with the times. We have seen the Internet radically change consumer buying habits and watched as many entrepreneurs successfully learned this new way of selling.

Another threat is the introduction of substitute products that could affect your business. Copycat products are easily created, and with the increase in

Chinese imports less expensive but similar products are hard to distinguish from the real thing.

Things can also happen internally that will affect your pricing strategy. An increase in fixed and variable costs will either diminish your profits or cause you to raise your prices. One particular vulnerable factor is transportation costs. Delivery and handling costs seem to be constantly inflating as oil prices fluctuate. Keep an eye on the fluctuating cost of a barrel of oil as cited on daily financial reports. Chaos in the Middle East or a natural disaster will cause immediate increases in the fuel cost of transportation and delivery services.

If there is a disruption in supply, costs will spiral. Whether it is food shortages caused by weather conditions or industry strikes, be prepared to find alternative suppliers in case of emergency.

Distribution

The logistics of distribution can be an integral factor in determining the pricing strategy of a business. Manufacturers in particular need to study the best way of moving their product to their customer. They need to determine the most efficient and effective channel of distribution for their particular product and industry.

There are four channels of distribution. (See also figure 10.2.)

1. Sell directly to their consumer through their own sales force or Internet website. It is the simplest and least costly channel but may not reach a large enough market.
2. Selling directly to retailers will expand the market and distribution of the product. This requires exhibiting at trade shows and possibly traveling to retail accounts, which of course drives up expenses; this is in addition to selling to the retailers at prices that allow them to sell at a suitable profit margin. These costs can be offset by manufacturing in larger production runs which will bring down the production cost per unit. This is termed economies of scale.

3. Selling through wholesalers will reach a larger market and works well for the business owner who wishes to distribute nationally and internationally without storing the goods in their location. The wholesaler will buy in large quantities and break down the bulk orders into parcels suitable for selling to small companies. However, it will add an additional middleman who will need to purchase at a price that allows selling to retailers who in turn sell to the final consumer.

4. The international business may wish to engage the services of agents to handle sales in different parts of the world. This involves an arrangement in which the company normally gives the agent much latitude on how to find and sell to customers in their native land. Often the agent takes possession of the goods and stores them in their locale. They are very similar to wholesalers but located outside the domestic borders of the manufacturer. International transportation fees and customs duties will add to the cost of product.

Figure 10.2
Channels of Distribution

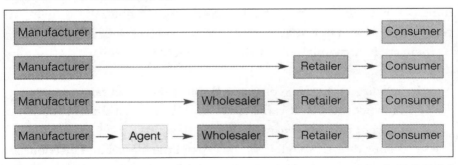

From *Moorman/Halloran. Successful Business Planning for Entrepreneurs (with CD-ROM), 1E. ©2006 South-Western, a part of Cengage Learning, Inc. Reproduced by permission.*

Epilogue

Ron did find a better way. It was apparent there was no way to compete with this type of large discount businesses with his budget limitations. He had to become more unique, more focused on a niche market, but what? He started by carefully examining the product selection at the discount operation— what didn't they have or what didn't they offer? Their product selection was larger and cheaper but the service was not as knowledgeable. But that was not enough to overcome the savings to his customers. What else could he do service-wise? Delivery and installation. He knew from helping so many customers over the phone the complications of setting up a sound system. Whether it was just to add a $50 speaker to an existing sound system or to install a $2,000 home music system, he would offer for himself or one of his sales/service professionals to come to the home or office and do the installation. His customers were delighted. In addition, he discovered that it led to additional sales of connecting cables and other smaller components that previously he had lost to neighborhood hardware stores. This allowed him to offer a unique service without raising prices. It also created a closer customer relationship that over the years would pay off in repeat sales.

Closing Tips

In determining your prices review the following:

1. Make sure the price covers the four essential points of cost of product, cost of operation, a fair profit to the owner, and a return on investment in order to reinvest and grow the business.
2. Determine the number of units at what price will be needed to break even.
3. Carefully review the prices of your competition.
4. Check with industry sources on what pricing strategies have worked well for their customers.
5. If desirable, experiment with introductory pricing strategies to see what works. Keep in mind that it is easier to lower prices at a later date than to raise them unless the discounts are clearly stated as temporary.
6. Scan the business environment for any external or internal factors that might disrupt your pricing strategy.

PART III

Taking the Yellow Brick Road?

The common pitfalls do not have to happen. Here are four stories of those who skipped the problems and went on to considerable success. That is not to say they made no errors but when they did, it was not due to their negligence. These entrepreneurs followed proper guidelines which allowed them to move through the opening steps much easier and with less expense. As you read the stories, put yourself in their position and ask what you would do in this situation. You should be able to identify with them because they were just like you in accepting the challenge and taking the risk.

It Couldn't Be Done

Somebody said that it couldn't be done
But he with a chuckle replied
That "maybe it couldn't," but he would be the one
Who wouldn't say so til he tried
So he buckled right in with the trace of a grin
On his face. If he worried he hid it.
He started to sing as he tackled the thing
That couldn't be done, and he did it.

There are thousands to tell you it cannot be done,
There are thousands to prophesy failure,
There are thousands to point to you, one by one
The dangers that await to assail you.
But just buckle in with a bit of a grin,
Just take off your coat and go to it:
Just start to sing as you tackle the thing
That "cannot be done," and you'll do it.
—*Edgar Guest*

11

The Right Start

The Idea

"O H YEAH, HERE WE GO AGAIN, PHIL HAS ANOTHER ONE OF HIS GET RICH quick ideas." Phil was surrounded by his weekly golf buddies at the 19th hole bar.

"Go ahead and laugh, you guys, but this time I'm serious. Why wouldn't miniature golf combined with a driving range, batting cages, trampolines, and an archery center work in this town? There is a definite lack of things to do for families and teenagers. If we offer all of these at one place there is something for everybody."

"Phil, the last miniature golf course in town lasted less than a year, both golf courses have driving ranges and what happens when winter sets in? It's another one of your 'I hate my job escape ideas.' Get serious."

"Ben, you are the biggest pessimist I know. That miniature golf course was doomed from the beginning—bad location, bad management, and boring holes. Sure, it will be seasonal, but our Georgia weather is not so severe that we would have to close down for winter. What about you Tim? You've been around here all your life."

"Well, you are right about the lack of things for families and kids to do, but what you are talking about takes some big bucks and I don't think you will find much money available in this economy. Banks are tight as can be. Ask Robbie, he's the college professor."

Robbie was trying his best to stay out of the conversation. Being a university business professor did not make him an expert on starting a business, and after shooting his worst score of the summer, he was in no mood to hear the old "those who can do, those who can't teach" routine that his friends so fondly liked to throw at him. "I'm not the guy to ask, but if you are serious you should call Betsy Garner over at our Small Business Development Center. There is no charge for her counseling and she has helped a lot of small business owners."

Ben chimed back in, "Forget it, Phil. You have a good job even if you are bored as hell. This is not the time to be taking risks. I'll bet Joanne would have a fit if she thought you were even considering quitting your job and going ahead on this. Let's have one for the road—on Robbie, the loser again today."

The Start

Ben was not too far off regarding Joanne. After dinner and the kids had been put to bed, Phil brought up his idea.

"Phil, we have two kids and a mortgage to consider before you start thinking about jumping off a cliff and starting a business. I know you are not happy at your job but the timing is not good."

"Honey, it is not that risky, I know what I'm doing. I have been consulting with entertainment businesses for ten years and I think I know what the market wants. Remember when everyone thought Westwood Amusement Park was going to go under, but I worked with them and they turned it around."

"But that was not your business, it was someone else's and that makes a difference," Joanne countered. "It is much easier to take risk with someone else's money than yours. We can't survive on my teacher's salary."

"I would not do it without making sure it would work. Robbie gave me the name of the gal at the university that heads up their Small Business

Development Center. She should be able to give me some feedback on the feasibility of the idea. I would at least like to run the idea past her."

"Look Phil, I know that you have always wanted your own business and I love your ambition and desire. I guess seeing this small business expert can't hurt; just make sure you don't get carried away."

Three days later Phil, equipped with some basic sketches and notes, showed up for a 9 A.M. appointment with Betsy Garner. He was received warmly and offered a cup of coffee. "Phil, Robbie Benson told me you were a friend of his. Robbie and I have worked on a few projects together and he is a very bright business person. He is a great guy to have in your corner."

"Let me tell you what we do here. We are here to help small businesses whether they are in the start-up phase or need assistance with problem solving. Small Business Development Centers are a form of partnership between the state university system and the Small Business Administration. We have a staff of counselors who have either small business experience or relevant academic or corporate backgrounds. These professionals are available at no charge for counseling and also lead various low-cost seminars here on campus and throughout the state in an effort to help our economy by helping small businesses. I believe you will find that you have come to the right place."

"Now tell me what you are up to and I will tell you how we can be of assistance."

Phil outlined his ideas, including showing some rough drawings of the layout of the family entertainment center.

"Very creative thinking, Phil, but you have got your work cut out for you for an idea this big. It will be costly, which means risky. I'm going to give you an agenda of things to work on before you invest one dollar. Any start-up business requires market research, and in your case rather extensive market research. I am sure you know what a business plan is, but have you ever done one for a start-up business?"

"No, Betsy, but I have a good deal of experience working with medium-size businesses solving problems and I am pretty knowledgeable about the entertainment industry."

"Okay Mr. Entrepreneur, let's get started. Here is a package of information regarding business plan writing and possible resources available. You will also see in there seminars we offer on a regular basis here at the university. As a matter of fact we have an all-day "How to Write a Business Plan" seminar a week from this Saturday. Can you make it?"

"Count on it, Betsy. Can I bring my wife? I want to get her involved."

"Great idea, Phil. She is more than welcome. Meanwhile, start your research. Our library is full of materials for you to use and the librarian will be glad to direct you. I am here to bounce ideas off of and offer suggestions but the work will fall on you. Why not come in the Monday after your seminar?"

Phil stood up and shook her hand, "Will do, Betsy, and thanks for the help."

Starting the Research

The first step in market research after identifying the question is to gather information. Phil spent hours in the library, searching the Internet at home in the evenings and making telephone inquiries. Except for Joanne he did not tell a soul about what he was doing—including Ben and Tim. Robbie did inquire as to whether he had seen Betsy, but Phil did not discuss the specifics of the meeting.

The first week he managed to write out a description of the business. It was only a page but it addressed all the related questions discussed in chapter 3. He identified the business as a family entertainment complex intended to serve the entire metropolitan area of Franklin, the county seat. He elaborated on his qualifications, citing seven years working as a consultant to theaters, sports organizations, and youth organizations. Although he could not be specific regarding location or operating schedule at this point, he indicated a preference to be in the center of the marketplace and with various operating hours depending on the season of the year. His short- and long-term goals were a combination of making a profit and providing the community with an asset. The competitive advantage of being the only business that would offer all these activities in one location was clearly and strongly stated.

Equipped with his description and his somewhat hesitant spouse, Phil attended the Small Business Development Center seminar. He learned much in regard to how to perform the next steps of his research and the proper format of the final plan. Good speakers, including Betsy, shared stories and lessons. They met others pursuing their dreams and felt a camaraderie with them by the end of the day. Even Joanne started to warm up to the idea and began contributing ideas and offers of assistance. For the first time they shared their business description with others and were quite pleased with the reception it received.

Betsy was also quite complimentary when she read the description at their meeting on Monday. She pointed out a few minor changes in wording and parts that needed some elaboration, but her overall evaluation was quite affirmative. "Good start, Phil, now are you ready for the hard stuff? The market analysis is going to determine if the market is big enough and economically sound enough to support the concept. You will be hitting the library quite a bit in determining the market demographics. Hopefully you can also tap into some of your industry contacts for support and quantitative data. Take your time and do this right because it will go a long way in determining an initial sales forecast."

The Demographic Study

During the next two weeks Phil was all over the place performing his market research. The search led him to the university library, the public library, the Internet, the Chamber of Commerce, and to the telephone calling industry representatives. The amount of information gathered was rather astonishing.

Population. The population of the metropolitan area had been growing at a rate of 2 percent per year over the past ten years. It now topped 200,000.

Age. The median age was slightly lower than the national and state average age.

Employment and income. Unemployment had risen somewhat since 2008 but was still below the national and state percentage rate. Annual pay was just about even with the state average pay, as was the average household and per capita income.

Industry sales. Leisure and entertainment gross sales for the market were lower than the average of other metropolitan areas of the state and also below the industry regional sales average.

Competition. Not counting local movie theaters, there were nine other entertainment businesses: three bowling alleys, one miniature golf course, a roller skating rink, and three driving ranges all affiliated with golf courses. The only batting cages were on the campuses of the high schools and university. The local YMCA offered access to archery and trampolines.

Of the nine competitors cited, seven were considered direct competition as they were dependent on active family leisure activities, the same as Phil's plan. Two of the three bowling alleys were doing well but the third was outdated and poorly located. There were rumors that it was in danger of closing unless a buyer was found. The driving ranges were doing okay in regard to regular golfers but, as Phil discovered after taking a survey, they were not attracting the novice golfer. A family-friendly environment might entice the novice to pick up a golf club and give it a try. The downtown roller rink was an attraction for kids but was seldom used by adults. Phil did not consider the YMCA as direct competition because trampolines and archery were only a small segment of their activities. Likewise the movie theaters, although competing for the leisure dollars, were considered as a different classification in researching industry trends and revenues.

Location. The last section of the market analysis was the consideration of where to place the business. Phil knew how important accessibility was to an entertainment business. He studied maps and road traffic counts. He knew he needed a minimum of two acres to accommodate the activities plus parking. He also knew he needed to be centrally located, which created a problem—where to find two vacant acres in an active city environment. Phil narrowed it down to an abandoned used automobile lot with frontage on a main thoroughfare or a vacant field just a block off the thoroughfare behind a grocery store.

The population, age, employment, and income statistics looked positive for the business, as did the competitive field, but Phil was concerned regarding the lower industry sales for his potential market. Further research showed that one of the highest industry sales markets in the region was the market area right next to Phil's. In discussing this with those in the industry, primarily area sales representatives, he learned that the nearby area had many more entertainment sites than his. This actually proved to be a positive discovery. In a survey of potential customers Phil found out that many were traveling to the neighboring marketplace for entertainment due to the lack of venues in their marketplace. In following that lead, Phil learned from industry sources that a population of 200,000 people should support more than twice the number of entertainment outlets than were available in his metropolitan market. Since the rest of his research showed no negative impacts on the spending ability of the market inhabitants, this confirmed Phil's survey.

Putting this all together, Phil was able to generate a ballpark estimate of sales. The 200,000 population spent an average of $125 per capita on active commercial leisure activities. This would indicate a potential market of $2,500,000 annual revenues shared among the businesses. Although he would be one of nine active competitors, Phil believed that since he would be the only complete venue he was capable of gaining 50 percent market share or $1,250,000 annual sales if he was conveniently and centrally located. He considered this as conservative since he believed many potential customers would come from those who presently traveled to the neighboring market. He knew this was rough, but it was a starting point. Now the question turned to whether $1,250,000 revenues would produce enough profit to gain an attractive return on the large investment that it would take to create such a business.

Phil shared the information with Betsy and the industry representatives he had gotten to know. Betsy was impressed with his research but urged him to continue studying his location options because she felt the wrong choice could be the kiss of death for the venture. The industry representatives were also high on the findings and urged Phil to proceed. Of course, Phil recognized, they made their living selling the products he might be purchasing.

Marketing Strategy

It would take 50,000 customers spending an average of $25 per year to reach $1,250,000 in revenues. Phil realized some customers would come only once or twice per year and spend less than $25 but others might come monthly or weekly and spend much more. He determined his initial objective would be to attract an average of 4,000 customers per month or approximately 160 per day if the complex was open 25 days per month. Phil realized he would have to project seasonal cash flow projections since summer might be four times the volume of customers in winter and two times spring and fall. He pondered what marketing tools should be used to successfully attract and retain that many customers. The choices were numerous.

Newspaper ads. There was a daily newspaper that served the entire metropolitan area. It was a good newspaper, but like so many daily papers it was decreasing in readership. It might work for a big event like the grand opening, but its expense in correlation to its readership and circulation was not suitable for a complete advertising campaign.

Yellow pages. This was another diminishing tool with so many using the computer for business addresses and information. It was still a necessity but probably not worth more than an attractive listing.

Radio. There were three local radio stations, each targeting different markets. One was youth, the other two more generic. Radio stations were now competing with satellite radio programming, not to mention iPods and iTunes for listeners. However, a radio ad could be personalized, and certainly during drive-time hours it reached a sizable market. In addition, radio programming of local events such as high school football games would certainly attract listeners that could be Phil's customers. It was more affordable than newspaper, so Phil thought it might have a place in his advertising budget.

Internet. Creating a website is a must in today's market. How to effectively design it to attract customers and provide information is a challenge. Phil knew how to operate computers and software, but designing a website was not one of his talents. He did know others who were quite capable, and it was also an area that Joanne could be quite helpful. Since a website was visual and could show activity it was ideal for his business. He penciled it into his budget.

Television. After doing some research Phil was surprised that television was not out of the question. There were local cable stations that his business could use to show its products quite effectively. It too was visual, and like radio it covered some local sports events and might fit quite well into his marketing plan.

Direct mail. The leader of the SBDC seminar had stressed that direct mail pieces could be quite effective for small businesses. It was the one medium that could be one on one with a customer as they read the material. It could also be personalized in its salutation. Its mailing list would come primarily from the business's customer database, which would grow as the business grew. Brochures, letters, and invitations were communication pieces that Phil would definitely use after he was in operation.

Billboards. A medium that he had not given much thought to was one that started to grow in appeal as he researched. Properly placed on a major transportation artery, a billboard could draw attention and direct customers to the business's existence. Depending on cost and where he was located, billboard advertising needed to be considered.

Magazines. There was a local attraction magazine which could be particularly helpful in attracting area visitors. If placed in motel and hotel lobbies it could be a nice way to gain new customers.

From Phil's previous experience as a consultant, combined with his industry sources, he knew a business such as his should spend approximately 5 percent of annual revenues on advertising. In his case that would be $62,500 based on his sales projection of $1,250,000. Although it sounded like a handsome figure, when he reviewed his options he realized it would be gone quite quickly if a good advertising plan could not be developed.

After researching all costs and circulations he arrived at the following plan.

Website design, hosting, and search fees—$10,000
Television (high school football and basketball games)—$8,000
Radio (sports talk shows and high school sports)—$7,000
Yellow pages—$2,000
Billboards (two at $4,000 each)—$8,000
Newspapers (special promotions only)—$5,000
Direct mail (brochures, promotion letters, etc.)—$12,000
Promotions (contests, special events)—$6,000
Reserve—$5,000

In addition, Phil budgeted $15,000 as a one-time-only cost for a grand opening weekend promotion. He would feature entertainment, food, beverages, and prizes with heavy advertising in newspaper and radio.

Betsy was impressed and gave him some advice. "Phil, a good marketing plan has to have a calendar. You need to make sure your advertising and promotions are spread throughout the year. Too many businesses jump in and out of the advertising market on a whim. Being in front of your customers consistently pays big dividends in the long term. Now it is time to rough out your management and human resource plan."

The Management Plan

Putting together a management plan was not difficult as Phil applied his years of experience as a marketing consultant to entertainment businesses. Although he had primarily worked with theatrical companies and amusement parks, he thought he knew what type of personnel to hire and what kind of management tools could be utilized in directing a profitable operation. He drew up an organization chart showing himself as manager with the help of an assistant manager. He divided the organization into the five different revenue sources of the business (miniature golf, driving range, trampoline, archery, and batting cages) and would assign a full-time head person for each area, supported by part-time positions to fill in when the full-time person was not available and during the busy weekend hours. He was hopeful that he could find personnel with some above-average abilities in the area assigned because they would then be able to assist with techniques to improve the customers' abilities and further enhance their satisfaction. The hours of operation would be Tuesday through Sunday 11 A.M. until 9 P.M. If the winter season proved to be too slow he would shorten some of the weekday hours.

The choice of operating systems, whether accounting or inventory control, was a matter of choosing what software Phil was most comfortable working with. Insurance policies were not so easy, as the liability factors of such a venture pushed the premiums up quite a bit. Several agents were contacted and asked for input. Suppliers of equipment and merchandise would be found at an upcoming trade show, but Phil already was gaining a feel for who was most helpful to him during the research phase.

The Legal Plan

The most important legal consideration was the type of ownership structure the business would operate under. A proprietorship was the easiest to form and keep records, but a lawyer who was consulted quickly pointed out that this business had liability considerations and the owner needed to be protected against outlandish liability suits. Proprietorships and partnerships are personally liable for all business activities, which meant that Phil could possibly lose all of his personal assets if there was an accident on the property and the suit was more than his insurance would cover. Phil had heard enough about frivolous lawsuits that he was not about to take the gamble. The lawyer suggested either form a corporation or a limited liability company. Both of these types of organization operated under their own individual identity with the same rights of a business owner. In case of a suit the plaintiff would sue the company and not the individual who worked for the company, thus protecting the individual's private property. Although it required some additional tax reporting forms and a registration fee it was a relatively inexpensive insurance policy for the owner(s).

There was an annual occupancy license requirement from the city or county. Since the business would not be serving food except for vending machines, a food license and health inspection were not necessary. The lawyer recommended that Phil check with his insurance provider to determine if a "not responsible declaration" was needed for trampoline or archery customers. Land purchase or lease contracts would be looked at as the opportunity occurred. Zoning regulations were not a problem as both locations were zoned for commercial use.

In addition to a lawyer, Phil also knew he needed an accountant to make sure he was in compliance with all federal and state tax regulations.

The plan was really starting to come together. Phil was excited. So was Joanne, but she was much more cautious. Both signed up for additional seminars at the university, including one entitled Raising Capital for a New Business. Betsy cautioned him that he might be excited now, but after researching the financial picture his enthusiasm might diminish.

The Financial Plan

Betsy knew what she was talking about. Two days into working on the financial plan Phil was about ready to concede defeat. All of his excitement was rapidly disappearing as he learned more about what the investment required. From his past experience he knew it would require a good bit of money, but he had not looked closely at the details.

He started by listing the one-time-only cost of getting the center opened. The land purchase would be approximately $90,000, which was not bad considering he had opted for the better location of the used car lot, which also had a small hut on the property which he could use as a customer check-in station and office.

The rest of the cost skyrocketed:

Miniature golf layout and equipment—$160,000
Driving range—$90,000
Lighting, grading, and landscape—$40,000
Batting cages (4) with pitching machines—$16,000
Trampoline (4)—$3,300
Archery equipment and inventory—$10,600
Grand opening—$15,000
Operating reserve fund—$10,000
Miscellaneous—$5,000
Total one-time-only cost—$439,900

"Wow," thought Phil, "twice what I thought it would be—impossible." A restless night followed as he and Joanne wrestled with what might have been.

"Can't we cut anything?" Joanne lamented.

"Only if we cut out some of the activities. I guess the archery center could come later and maybe one of the batting cages. The elimination of these would cost us about 10 percent of our projected sales. The landscape budget could be cut by maybe $10,000, This would get it down close to $400,000, which is still way over our heads. We only have $60,000 and no bank is going to loan us almost $350,000. I will see if Betsy has any ideas but I am not optimistic."

Betsy was not as pessimistic. "Difficult," she said, "but not impossible depending on the profit potential. Run a projected profit and loss and then let's see how it looks."

Phil ran some numbers for estimated operating costs.

Cost of materials—$25,000 (golf balls, scorecards, etc.)
Utilities—$95,000
Insurance—$18,000
Payroll—$195,000 (including Phil's salary at $60,000)
Payroll taxes—$12,500
Maintenance—$18,000
Advertising—$62,500
Accounting, legal—$6,000
Supplies—$24,000
Miscellaneous—$50,000
Total estimated annual operating cost—$506,000

"Betsy, this is pretty good if we take in $1,250,000. I know it does not include any interest costs or principal reduction, but there is room here. If we borrowed or begged $350,000, the interest would be around $25,000 a year and principal payment over 5 years would be $70,000 each year. We would still have a cushion of over $600,000. Is this possible?"

"Remember Phil, you still have taxes to pay and money to be put aside for depreciation allowance to replace worn-out equipment. Try being a little more conservative in your projection; remember, you have dropped the archery center and insert the debt and taxes and see how it looks."

Phil lowered his sales projection 25 percent and subtracted out the additional debt payout of $95,000 and plugged in $155,000 for taxes and arrived at a final figure showing a surplus of approximately $195,000. Still a very encouraging picture if he could only find $350,000.

"Write up your business plan into a formal proposal and take it to the bank, Phil, it can't hurt to try. If they say no ask them if they would be willing to participate in sponsoring you for a Small Business Administration loan. It is still a bank note, but if approved the bank will be guaranteed up to 90 percent of the loan by the SBA in the event you default."

A week later Phil was sitting in Hank McGuire's office at the bank answering a million questions regarding his business plan. Hank was impressed by the business plan and told Phil he would take it to the loan committee but not to be too optimistic, as loaning $350,000 of a $400,000 investment was very unusual. He would also inquire as to whether the bank would do an SBA loan.

Two weeks later they met again.

"Phil, we can get you $200,000 if you can raise the other $150,000 but that's about as far as we can go. There is no problem loaning against the property purchase and using some of the equipment as collateral, but anything else would be unsecured and we just don't do that for a start-up business with no history. The SBA would be a possibility, but they are pretty snowed under at this time and it will take at least six weeks to get an answer. These days most of their efforts are aimed at helping businesses working in economically distressed areas of the economy, so I don't know how they would appraise an entertainment complex."

Phil left the bank thinking $150,000 might as well be two million. It appeared hopeless. Joanne tried to console him but he was exasperated and tired of the whole thing. Two weeks later Phil confessed the whole story to his golfing buddies. " I told you Phil," said Ben. Stay with your job. You don't need this agony. Give up on your crazy ideas and be happy with what you have."

Tim concurred. "Remember, I told you the banks wouldn't cooperate. Your timing is not good."

Robbie offered his sympathy and as before said little but that evening he called Phil at home. "Phil, I work with a group of fellows who invest in small businesses. This little venture group might be interested if you are willing to turn over a portion of ownership and profits to them if successful. I have referred a couple of businesses to them through the business school and will do the same for you if interested. You would be the majority owner, they would just share in a percentage of profits"

"Why not?" thought Phil, "60 percent of profits is better than 100 percent of nothing." "Sure Robbie, set it up, and thanks." A lawyer drew up a private stock offering which showed the investor group with 40 percent ownership, which allowed Phil to keep full control of the business operation.

The next three weeks were spent working out the details and tweaking the profit and loss projections. Betsy was very helpful and even accompanied him to the meeting. It went perfectly and six months later Phil opened FAMILY FUNTIME to a very enthusiastic audience. The business was successful. Although Phil scraped through on a sparse salary for a couple of years, he emerged in grand fashion and three years later bought out his investors, who also did quite well.

12

Think Marketing

MARY ELLEN HAD JUST FINISHED WRITING A NOTE OF GRATITUDE TO HER former entrepreneurship professor. He had been so right. It was her restaurant's one-year anniversary and she was giving herself a well-deserved pat on the back for its success, but she also wanted to share her success with Professor Norling. So much of what he had preached had come to reality, particularly the importance of developing a successful marketing plan. She recalled the story and the lesson that was behind his lecture on the importance of being involved in all the marketing decisions and not leaving them to the so-called professionals. After all, the entrepreneur knows his or her business and their customers better than the advertisement salesperson or illustrator. These people are there to assist the entrepreneur but not to create the message. The following story he told validated the message.

The owner of an automobile dealership was not satisfied with his sales results. He decided that he would attend a taping for a new, but very familiar themed, television ad showing a new car and glamorous young lady telling how the car had made her life so exciting. The ad was very similar to all the ads he and most of his competitors had run in the past—a flashy car and a flashy spokesperson touting the benefits of ownership. The more he watched the production the more frustrated he became. Finally he arose from his chair and exclaimed "Stop, can't we do something new and show something with some imagination?"

The ad producer looked up from his camera. "But this is the going thing, why change it?"

"Because it is not working, that's why. My customers are bored to death with this approach. I know what they want and they want action. Let me give you an example."

With that he jumped on the hood of the car and exclaimed "I want to sell you a car!" and proceeded to tell them how they could own a car such as this instead of just dreaming about it. He was surprised that as he got down from the car, the film crew started clapping. The producer was astounded. "That was great. We were still running the cameras when you jumped on the car, come see yourself at your greatest."

After viewing the tape the auto dealer felt a little sheepish about his rather outlandish demonstration but was pleased with the excitement it caused. He asked the producer, "Do you think you can find the right person to do that ?"

"YOU are the right person to do that. Only you can show that passion. It is your business and it comes through loud and clear that you can help them buy that car."

It took some persuasion, but it was agreed that he would do the ad and it took off. Its creatively caused so much stir that the dealership's ad was featured on a late night national television show. Sales soared and a year later had more than doubled. It seemed everyone wanted to meet the crazy guy who screamed "I want to sell you a car." The lesson learned was the importance of injecting owner input into advertising and not taking the easy path.

Professor Norling had made his point and Mary Ellen had learned an important rule. It was her business and she knew her customers and her products better than an outsider and she would make all the marketing decisions. Any ad or marketing promotion run reflects the image of the business and consequently the image of the owner.

Mary Ellen's Marketing Plan

Mary Ellen knew that it all started with the first impression—in this case the grand opening. What makes a successful grand opening promotion? Excitement and fun. It is the most important advertising campaign many businesses will ever do. It is their time to introduce themselves and make that very important first impression. Too many businesses treat it too lightly when, in fact, it has the ability to make or break a new business. The grand opening needs to be treated separately from any other promotions. It is a one-time expenditure and the resources to do it right must be available.

Mary Ellen reserved $6,000 to announce the grand opening of the Front Porch Restaurant. It was her opportunity to greet and meet her new customers. The first question was, what theme? The restaurant was a family-style eatery. The menu featured healthy meals, moderately priced. She combined numerous elements in order to appeal to all family members. They served wine and beer but not hard liquor. There were TVs located in the upper corners of the dining area for the sports fans. There were some kid's arcade tables in the foyer leading to the tables and plenty of crayons and challenge puzzles at the tables. A small gift shop offered travel items, magazines, and pick-me-up gifts and costume jewelry. It all spelled out family food and entertainment at a reasonable price; therefore that became the theme. She decided to open on a Sunday, a family day. Kids love superheroes so off to the costume store to dress some of her staff. A carnation for the moms would serve as a take-home reminder that all had fun. A barbershop quartet was there to add to the festivities. All entrees were half price. It was quite a Sunday afternoon for all.

Mary Ellen resisted the temptation to have a limited or soft opening, instead choosing to spend extra time training her staff until she felt confident they would pull it off without a hitch. After all, if you are not prepared to open full blast, you are not ready to open.

The cost was the equivalent of 33 percent of her annual advertising budget, but in hindsight it was worth every penny of it. For media she used the local daily newspaper. Although she was not planning on using newspapers as her primary advertising medium, an event this big would attract people from all over town and needed broad exposure. The cost of a 3 × 8 column inch ad, approximately one half page, in the local/entertainment section was $1,080. She supported this with radio ads, three 30-second spots per day on two stations during drive time for the five days leading up to the Sunday at a cost of $900. She also used direct mail postcards to over 10,000 homes in the closest zip code, cost $2,400. The barbershop quartet was $800, the costumes $300, and the extra help and giveaways were $700. Expensive, but it was effective as it filled all the tables, all day long. There was a waiting line at times during the afternoon, but customers did not seem to mind as they were entertained by the quartet and superheroes. What really made it stand out as a success was the photo of the mayor cutting the ribbon that accompanied an article in the paper the following day. Mary Ellen had the foresight to personally invite the mayor in hopes that he would bring the publicity.

She recalled Professor Norling advising that retail stores, including restaurants, were social institutions. They go to restaurants or shopping malls to get out of the home, to have fun and be entertained. The primary objective of the grand opening is not sales. The right grand opening experience creates goodwill and the desire to comeback. Any extra sales are an added bonus to that. Treat it as a grand social event. Entertain, feed, demonstrate, all with the objective of sending the attendee home talking to others about the new business in town. Word-of-mouth advertising is the most effective advertisement a business can achieve.

The First-Year Advertising Calendar

Mary Ellen reviewed her first-year marketing calendar. She had established a budget of $18,000 (6 percent of sales). The budget was to cover all advertising, promotional events, and public relations activities.

The first-year advertising plan had pretty much stayed on course and been effective by following the basic tenets of advertising.

Be consistent. In other words, don't blow your whole budget on just a few events. Spread the program over the entire year to keep yourself in the public eye. It was okay to put more emphasis on certain seasons or events, but not at the expense of disappearing from view at other times of the year.

A good ad must achieve fulfillment of the acronym AIDA, which stands for Attention, Interest, Desire, and Action. To be effective the ad must capture the audience's attention, create their interest in the product or service, build desire for the product or service, and lastly ask for action, that is, "Buy Now," "Come in Today." Professor Norling had emphasized that this was not easy. Fighting for attention in competition with others in our fast-paced society could be very expensive. Once attention was gained, how do you entice the audience to read or listen on? The comprehension of the ad must build a desire for its benefits and finally, remind them to act at once. Once the desire has been built it can quickly disappear if not acted on promptly. The Action part was often the one most neglected by advertisers. Mary Ellen noticed that many ads of her competitors did not ask for action.

Keep it simple was an ironclad commandment. Exposure time to readers and listeners was very short. Do not be guilty of information overload. This was often expressed in the acronym KISS, Keep It Simple, Stupid. The "stupid" was there to remind the advertisers of the mistake of overloading.

Do not waste money by overreaching your marketplace. Be realistic in your ability to draw customers. Do not pay for advertisements that are circulated 50 miles from your business unless it serves a niche that customers will drive an hour to get to you. In such a situation you are paying as much to entice that customer as you are the customers who live in your immediate marketplace.

Running ads too much in advance will not be effective. The customer has a short memory. Inviting them to a sale or event two weeks beforehand will not work. Ads should be designed for more immediate action. Depending on the event or product, ads that run more than two days in advance are normally not effective.

Make sure your ad or event fits your business stage in the life cycle. Businesses and products go through four stages: introductory, growth, maturity, and decline. Each of these stages requires a different approach to marketing. The Front Porch was initially in the introductory or pioneering stage so the advertising campaign should emphasize "new." After a few months the restaurant would enter the growth or competitive stage in which it could exclaim its superiority over the competition. The Front Porch was a long way from the maturity or retentive stage, but the day would come when it would need to re-create its image to stay current. Eventually it would face decline, but hopefully on positive terms and not because of poor marketing conditions. At that point Mary Ellen would use her marketing campaigns to forestall her exit until the time was right.

So keeping these lessons and her budget in mind she designed a monthly advertising calendar.

January: Campaign #1: *New Year's Day Dinner,* ¼ page newspaper one time, 20 radio spots. Campaign #2: *The Holidays Are Over, Let Mom Out of the Kitchen,* ¼ page newspaper 3 times, 10 radio spots per week = total monthly budget $1,200

February: Campaign #1: *A Special Valentine Dinner,* ¼ page newspaper one time, 20 radio spots the week prior to Valentine's Day = total monthly budget $500

March: Campaign #1: *St Patrick's Day Special,* ¼ page newspaper one time, 10 radio spots Campaign #2: *Welcome Spring Daily Specials* ¼ page newspaper two times, 20 radio spots. Total monthly budget = $1,000

April: Campaign #1: *Easter Feast,* ¼ page newspaper one time, 20 radio spots. Campaign # 2: *Welcome Spring Daily Specials,* ¼ page three times, 30 radio spots. Total monthly budget = $1,200

May: Campaign #1: *Mother's Day Brunch* ¼ page newspaper one time, 20 radio spots. Campaign #2: *Graduation Celebration* ¼ page newspaper two times, 20 radio spots. Total monthly budget = $1,200

June: Campaign #1: *Take Dad Out for Dinner,* ¼ page newspaper one time, 20 radio spots. Campaign #2: *Summer Daily Specials* ¼ page newspaper one time, 20 radio spots. Total monthly budget = $ 1,000

July: Campaign #1: *Celebrate Fourth of July,* ¼ page newspaper one time, 20 radio spots. Campaign #2 *Summer Daily Specials,* 40 radio spots. Total monthly budget = $800

August: Campaign #1: *Back to School Shoppers Rest Stop*, ¼ page newspaper two times, 40 radio spots. Campaign #2 *Summer Daily Specials*, 40 radio spots. Total monthly budget = $800

September: Campaign #1: *Welcome Fall Specials*, ¼ page newspaper four times, 40 radio spots. Total monthly budget = $1,200

October: Campaign #1: *Football Tailgate Specials*, ¼ page newspaper two times, 40 radio spots. Total monthly budget = $800

November: Campaign #1: *Fall Specials*, ¼ newspaper page three times, 30 radio spots. Campaign #2 *Thanksgiving Dinner Banquet*, ¼ newspaper page one time, 20 radio spots. Total monthly budget = $1,200

December: Campaign #1: *Christmas Shoppers Specials*, ¼ newspaper page four times, 60 radio spots. Campaign #2 *Enjoy Christmas Dinner at The Front Porch*, ¼ page newspaper one time, 20 radio spots. Total monthly budget = $1,500

Of course, an advertising program would not be complete without a website and taking advantage of social media. Mary Ellen secured the Internet domain site www.frontporchrestaurant.com and featured it prominently on all of her advertising. She knew enough about computers that she designed the site herself and made sure it was easy to change by season or different messages. She also linked it to the Chamber of Commerce website. She also became very familiar and active with Facebook and LinkedIn.

Total media advertising was budgeted at $12,500. That left $5,500 available for promotional events and public event activities.

The Promotion Calendar

Mary Ellen learned over the year that promotional events were not only good business but were also fun for customers and staff. She decided early on that the number one promotional event would be The Front Porch Birthday Club.

By getting customers to fill out a birthday card reminder she was able to collect names and addresses of valuable customers—the start of the very important customer database. She would use this list to send out a happy. birthday greeting one week before the event which offered a free birthday dinner entree. They also received special attention as birthday guests when they arrived, including a song and free after-dinner cake. Although the cost of the greeting cards, cakes, and mailings amounted to $1,500 it produced significant sales and more importantly built customer loyalty.

In addition Mary Ellen decided to hold four special events each year. One such event was a kids night featuring free desserts, a clown, and a magician. It cost $800, including extra advertising costs.

Fashion night was also a big hit. Various local fashion boutiques were invited to bring models and hold a fashion show. The evening ended with raffle for $1,000 fall wardrobe. The cost was primarily borne by the stores except for $300 in refreshments.

Closely related to this was a Bride's Night in early March in which bridal fashions were displayed by models from the various bridal shops. Mary Ellen's share of the refreshment and advertising cost was $400.

During the Christmas season there was an evening of holiday storytelling complete with Santa Claus. Lots of giveaways and treats for the kids at a cost of $1,000.

Without exception the promotions were successful and created exactly what Mary Ellen had hoped for—fun and goodwill and even some extra sales. The total budget for all promotions was $4,000.

Public Relations

Mary Ellen knew that if she was to continue for the long term she needed to contribute back to the community. It was the ethical thing to do, and in the long term the goodwill generated would pay off in customer loyalty.

It was impossible to contribute to every organization and cause that requested help in the community. Mary Ellen had to pick and choose as to which of these causes she thought would benefit the most. Certainly the United Way was one. She had a personal history with the Boys and Girls Club and wanted to support it. Her oldest son was playing Little League baseball, so she felt an obligation to support his team as a sponsor. Then there was the community theater, the Salvation Army, the hospital auxiliary, and the many school clubs. She budgeted $1,500 for community donations but also contributed many free meals and her time. She joined service organizations and the Chamber of Commerce and became active in many community events. Anytime she was pictured in a community event it also served as good public relations for The Front Porch.

Although her budget was spent, Mary Ellen was not finished with her marketing plan. She remembered distinctly Professor Norling's advice about securing free publicity. "Get to know your media people, they will become important." Newspaper reporters are always on the lookout for stories of public interest. It was also a fact that some days they needed help in finding good subjects to write about. An interesting business was always good copy. Mary Ellen learned that food was one of those subjects. Therefore when she had a new entree that was not well known, the newspaper would sometimes feature it in a food-related article and often with a photo. Her promotional events also sometimes made good stories, particularly if they featured children. The holiday storytelling evening made front page in the community section of the local newspaper and was featured on local television news programming. And all it cost was a phone call to a friend at the newspaper.

Effective Selling

Mary Ellen had never thought there was a correlation between selling and restaurants. What are you selling to restaurant customers that is not listed on a menu? Image and goodwill.

Every customer who enters a restaurant wants to feel appreciated and wanted. They not only want good food but expect good service. A pleasant smile, assistance with food choice, conversation, all build image and relationships which in turn produce satisfied customers which produces sales.

Mary Ellen arranged extensive training sessions with her staff. She hired outside resources to teach restaurant etiquette and the proper approach.

They role-played, read articles, and participated in computer training sessions. She recognized that the menu was a sales tool and spent hours agonizing over the right look and assortment of food selection.

Personal selling started with a welcome and did not end until there was a satisfied customer. Even in a restaurant it followed the selling process of approach, presentation, handling objections, closing the sale, and follow-up. It was just a much more subtle sale than the more obvious situation. A customer did not leave The Front Porch Restaurant without a compliment and an inquiry as to their degree of satisfaction. Suggestion cards were on every table.

Staff training was ongoing. Every three months Mary Ellen brought the staff together for a practice training session. She also awarded staff for service above and beyond, sometimes with bonuses and more often with a gift which served as a take-home reminder of their exceptional work.

There was no doubt about the first year's success of the Front Porch. But could she keep it going? It seemed that every day there was new competition. Many did not last, but all competed for market share. The secret would lie not just in her product but very much in her future marketing plans. Attracting new customers and retaining old customers was an ongoing challenge. Mary Ellen had learned the value of Professor Norling's advice of controlling her marketing activities herself and not turning them over to others. She would have to keep up her marketing enthusiasm and stay abreast of new communication technologies, but that should not be a problem because "marketing was fun."

13

Teamwork Works

"OKAY EVERYONE, DINNER AT NATALIE'S IS ON ME," GREGG ANNOUNCED TO his crew of six. Another successful month—the fifth in a row of beating the sales objective. What a change from two years ago when it seemed all hell would break loose any minute of every day.

Two years ago Gregg bought out G&T Limited to increase his wholesale exposure. It was quite a step for a young business but it made sense. The only problem was that he inherited a group of dissatisfied workers. They had been poorly trained and were not motivated to lift a finger to go outside their basic job responsibilities. If 5 o'clock was quitting time they were packing to go at 4:30 and out the door at five no matter what was on the table at the time. It was no wonder G&T was willing to sell at a lowball price. Their business was doing as poorly as their employees.

Gregg had made great progress with his jewelry and accessory import business. First with retail Internet sales and then he moved into the wholesale arena. In the beginning it was he and his wife Shannon traveling from merchandise market to merchandise market as temporary exhibitors. The large metropolitan merchandise marts were occupied by permanent wholesaler and manufacturer showrooms which were open year-round, but during the seasonal trade shows temporary exhibitors like Gregg were invited for a hefty cost to set up their displays and meet with prospective customers.

The reception of Gregg's business had been good but the profits limited. He could only go so far with his limited line of goods so he started to search for the missing piece. He found his niche when he started to experiment with leather goods. The leather goods included everything from fashion handbags and men's billfolds to belts, briefcases, and fashionable computer carry-on cases. It all fit in quite well with his jewelry and accessory lines. Many of his current clientele sold leather goods as an add-on to Gregg's accessories. He started with just a few lines and did okay but the competition for floor space was intense. Many stores carried G&T Limited, although they were very dissatisfied with the service. Gregg made it a point to seek out the owner of G&T at the next trade show to investigate what they were planning in the future. He was surprised when the owner came right out and asked, "Would you be interested in buying us out? We are selling our inventory at cost if you are willing to take over the remainder of our permanent space lease in the Dallas merchandise mart." Gregg was interested. He could tell that G&T was struggling as it sounded like a desperate move. The risk was the two-plus years remaining on the merchandise mart lease, a very expensive proposition. It would add an entirely new dimension to his business and would take him from his mom and pop status into a million-dollar operation with full-time and part-time employees.

Negotiations proved to be successful and two months later Gregg was the proud owner of G&T, now renamed Fashion Plus Accessories. He had acquired inventory, a permanent merchandise mart showroom, and a small warehouse operation. He also now had eight employees in addition to himself and his wife. Three of them were salespeople, who worked the showroom and visited accounts on a regular basis, a bookkeeper who kept track of all invoicing, bills, and account records, and four warehouse workers who received inventory and packed outgoing orders. The problem of the poor worker performance became evident right from the beginning.

For starters, two would have to go to make room for Gregg and his wife. The previous owner had worked very little, therefore his everyday work input was discounted. The bookkeeper was let go and Janet took over those responsibilities. She was very glad to get off the road and Gregg was very glad to have someone he could trust handle the very important bookkeeping responsibilities. The books were a mess. Months of neglect left Janet with a challenging catch-up assignment. She consulted with a CPA who set her up and trained her on a very tailored bookkeeping software program. Within thirty days she was on the way to creating an accurate and up-to-date system that would keep her and Gregg informed on a daily basis as to how they were doing in regard to budgeting, sales, cash flow, and meeting objectives.

The other position that had to go was the warehouse foreman, a man who had long ago lost interest in his job and was very difficult to work with. Gregg would temporarily assume his responsibilities along with supervising the sales activities of the showroom, visiting accounts, and continuing exhibiting at other merchandise trade shows as a temporary exhibitor.

Those cuts took care of Gregg and Janet coming aboard, but he had to improve the employees' performance. He first reviewed the spotty records of the three saleswomen. None were particularly strong, but in particular the more experienced one who acted as the showroom supervisor was lacking in attitude, approach, and appearance. She was not punctual and her rapport with clients was not warm. The younger ladies, Lindy and Carol, had stronger selling qualities which showed in their sales results. They were both a bit rough around the edges, but Gregg believed that was due to poor training. He immediately started a sales training program. He was familiar with a very professional six-week computer training-assisted program. They would meet as a group of four, three mornings a week, to review lessons and practice through role playing. The other two days, the women would work with the computer training programs. Gregg could see the improvement with the younger women immediately as they really delved into the lessons. Their sales started to rise and he received compliments from clients regarding their improved approach and sales manners. The more experienced woman started on the right note but faded quickly. She approached Gregg a month after his arrival: "Gregg, this is not for me. I am not used to this kind of selling and in all honesty have no interest in learning new ways. I am leaving for an administrative job across town."

Gregg was relieved and he started a search for a replacement. He interviewed over ten applicants after advertising online and in a weekly trade journal. In the interview he made it a point not to overly glamorize the job but to speak honestly about opportunities. He stressed that although the starting pay and commissions were not high, as a new owner he was determined to grow the business and when that happened all would be rewarded. He had each applicant spend time with Lindy and Carol, as he wanted their opinion and at the same time it gave the candidate a more comprehensive view of the organization. When he got down to the best three candidates they were invited back individually for an informal lunch with himself, the saleswomen, and Jane to answer their questions and to get a better feel for each other. Gregg was more interested in personality and ambition than previous experience as he expected to train the new sales manager himself once that person had been hired.

Hiring decisions are one of the most important responsibilities of the entrepreneur. It is his or her role to build an enthusiastic team of workers who enjoy coming to work. The most stressful times an entrepreneur will encounter can come from personnel issues. Relationships can turn sour and workers can become lax. Taking all this into consideration, Gregg did not rush into the decision of hiring hastily. He eventually chose Elizabeth, a middle-aged woman with not as much experience as some of the other candidates but one who possessed an incredibly positive outlook on life. He would bring her on as his sales manager with hopes that her spirit would be contagious to all around her.

Gregg applied the same considerations and procedure in hiring a new shipping foreman. He was successful in hiring David, an individual with considerable shipping experience but more importantly a leader. A former military leader, David was ideal for the challenge of infusing discipline into the remaining three-member crew of the warehouse.

Gregg was intent on managing with a Theory Y, participative management style. He wanted to build, as much as possible, a family culture. Feeling confident that his new people felt the same, he delegated much authority to them. He held weekly meetings with the entire staff, which included the salespeople. The salespeople had never met with the warehouse personnel under the previous owner, which meant they had no understanding of the others' problems. Previously the two groups were adversaries, with sales blaming warehouse if orders did not ship in time and warehouse blaming sales for making impossible promises to customers. Now they began to understand each others' problems and harmony was achieved.

Sales Division

Although there were only three salespeople plus himself, Gregg recognized his group as a sales division. He was quite familiar with the organizing task of management in assigning tasks and dividing responsibilities. He appointed Elizabeth as the sales manager and Lindy and Carol as sales associates. Between the four of them they would man the permanent showroom five days per week, travel to retail stores when possible, and set up as temporary exhibitors in annual trade show in Atlanta, Chicago, New York, and Los Angeles. Their responsibilities also included telemarketing to potential customers. Sales training was held on a quarterly basis to stay up-to-date. Commissions were set slightly higher than the industry average to compensate for a somewhat below average salary with health and vacation benefits. In addition, there were sales contests after each training session, with emphasis on particular products. The contests were designed to be fun to participate in and not cutthroat. The winners received gifts, not cash. The gifts were something of use such as television sets, computers, or cameras. Cash prizes might cause competitive clashes which even when won would often just go into the family checking account to pay bills. Gifts were more permanent and would remind the recipient of their good work whenever used. After a time of introduction and familiarity, Lindy and Carol both accepted Elizabeth as their manager and her enthusiasm started to spill over into their attitudes. Three months into the new arrangement Gregg was delighted with the way the camaraderie was developing.

Shipping and Receiving

The warehouse crew was a little more complicated. David knew the job well, but his style was more military or Theory X than either Gregg or the workers were prepared for. When Gregg approached him regarding his direct authoritative style, David defended it by stating that the workers were lax and needed more discipline. Gregg had to admit this was very true and thought maybe some forced discipline might instill more pride in the job. He cautioned David to back off somewhat but did not tell him to completely move away from his style. There was one casualty six weeks into David's tenure as foreman when Marty, who had been with the company for three years, resigned, stating, "This is a far cry from the old days, you can take this job and the new boss and you know what you can do with it." Marty had been a complainer since day one of Gregg's arrival, and it had only gotten worse after David came on board. Gregg's thoughts that this might not be the worst thing to happen were confirmed when he noticed a new cohesiveness among the two remaining workers, Barry and Richie. He found out that they had not liked working with Marty and were pleased that he had left, and their work showed improvement. The improvement allowed David to back off from the authoritative management style and the team started to come together. Thursday evening beer treat became part of their culture at the tavern across the street. They became so productive that Gregg was able to hire just a part-time worker to fill in for Marty's hours.

Gregg also redesigned the jobs. Packing and unpacking shipments on a daily basis can get to be monotonous. Gregg redesigned the jobs by specialization and rotation. The four main jobs were (1) checking off and entering the shipments that were received or sent, (2) collecting the packing materials for outgoing goods and unloading the received goods, (3) loading and sealing the cartons to go and placing the incoming merchandise on the proper shelves and (4) loading the trucks and discarding the packaging materials. Each worker spent half of a shift on one assignment and then would move to the next for the second half of the shift. There was friendly competition among the worker of an activity on the first shift versus the worker who took over the assignment in the second shift. In addition, Gregg delegated the responsibility of scheduling and other decisions along to David, who

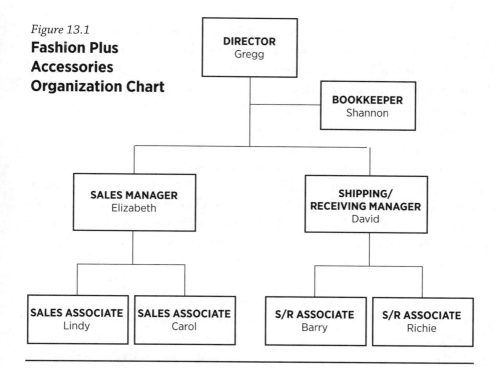

Figure 13.1

Fashion Plus Accessories Organization Chart

would consult closely with his team. This was a great departure from the way the previous warehouse system had operated. The workers were now involved and felt they were contributing to the health and wealth of the company. There was also a bonus system implemented that was paid on a quarterly basis if shipments left on time. (For an organization chart of the company as reorganized by Gregg, see figure 13.1.)

Setting Objectives

In a previous job Gregg had been victimized by a manager who set unrealistic objectives which created tension throughout the workforce when not reached. He was determined not to do the same.

Once he felt satisfied with his new staff and the ice was broken in regard to relationships, Gregg set out to meet with each employee separately to discuss objectives and opportunities. These meetings were held in a relaxed atmosphere either in the diner across the street after the lunchtime rush or in the employee break room. He gave each employee at least ten days' notice regarding having a meeting to individually discuss the future. Gregg brought with him some rather scanty performance reports left behind by the previous owner. He asked the employee to bring any suggestions or criticisms that they would like to discuss.

Each meeting started with a positive acknowledgment of the employee's contribution to the company. This was followed by Gregg's declaration of his hopes for the future, which allowed him to transition into the employee's individual hopes for their future. From this Gregg was able to fuse the two goals together. He made scant mention of the past since he had not been there and wanted all to feel it was a fresh start.

The discussion then proceeded to either shipping objectives or sales production goals for the coming year. Gregg knew there had to be improvement over past performance of the company or else he was doomed. Sales had to increase almost 20 percent to make a profit. It was not possible to assign all salespeople a 20 percent sales increase objective without setting off alarm and fear. Gregg figured his personal input and sales enthusiasm should result in some of that increase, allowing him to discuss achieving a 10 percent increase as an objective. He was willing to decrease that objective if the sales associate thought it unrealistic. This proved to be unnecessary as the sales force had been somewhat reenergized and were looking forward to the challenge of a written goal. Much of the energy stemmed from the promise of a bonus and possible raise if objectives were reached. Gregg was not specific as to the exact amount of financial incentive as he was too new to commit to a particular dollar reward, but he made it clear that he would be as generous as possible and would share with them the financial resources of the company. He also announced regular quarterly meetings, or sooner if necessary, to review progress to make sure all were on track or if help was needed to get them back on track. Each salesperson signed off on the agreement and was given a copy with an encouraging note from Gregg.

The objective meeting with the shipping and receiving group members was a bit more complicated. Sales could easily be calculated and measured but shipping was much more nebulous. Since assigning specific numbers to an individual's performance was not realistic, Gregg took more of a team approach. If the team could achieve getting orders out without delays or goods unpacked on the day of delivery they would earn points toward the objective. They could also receive individual points for pitching in extra when someone was absent and for on-time and perfect attendance. It amounted to a two-level performance appraisal system: a bonus for team goal achievement supplemented with individual work attitude and contribution. As with the sales force, Gregg promised quarterly meetings with each to review progress or determine if help was needed to achieve the objectives. All of the workers were pleased since they formerly had no bonus or appraisal system and they wanted to know how their work measured up to expectations. They too received a signed agreement and an encouraging note from Gregg one week following their meeting.

Building a Cohesive Team

Gregg clearly understood the value of teamwork. He had often heard the term *synergy*, meaning the whole is greater than its parts. A good cohesive team working together can accomplish more than the individual output of its members.

Small teams in particular have the ability to grow to greater productivity if morale is high and leadership is consistent. Gregg considered himself the leader of two teams, but at the same time the teams could merge together to reach organization objectives.

During the first few months he closely watched the teams coming together. Although the carryover associates had worked together before there was not a team environment. It was like starting anew. At the beginning there was a period of orientation and uncertainty with Lindy, Carol, Barry, and Richie stemming from the new organization and leadership from Gregg, Elizabeth, and David . The big questions were "What is acceptable?" "What is expected of me?" and "How will these changes affect me?" Gregg made sure there was time available for the associates to spend time together to get more acquainted in non-work situations, whether at coffee breaks or lunch periods. It did not take long for individual personalities to emerge and assume roles. There was of course some conflict as to roles, but as friendships developed cooperation became the accepted practice. After this stage, group norms developed which answered the question of what is acceptable. Barry learned from the facial expressions of David and Richie that coming in ten minutes late put more work and pressure on them. Carol backed off from her gossipy tales when she learned that Lindy and Elizabeth were not paying attention. It took time for all to feel comfortable in their roles, but with Gregg's open door policy there soon developed participation in setting goals and proposing ideas. With this harmony the leadership roles of David and Elizabeth emerged, allowing Gregg to step back into more of an organization versus a team leader role. Six months into the changes the teams were performing at an accelerated level. There was great cooperation and group problem solving. Task accomplishment became a source of pride.

Gregg felt he had accomplished building an interdependent group: a group that realized that working together was more efficient and enjoyable. This carried over into the two teams cooperating and coordinating together for the benefit of the organization. Team members became proactive by taking action in anticipation of problems instead of sitting back and waiting until they happened. They learned to focus on the end objective, not on just getting through the day. There was less time spent on performing superfluous activities as opposed to tasks that took priority. Win/win became a way of thinking. There was no sense selling fashion accessories to a customer whose store did not cater to the desired target market. Neither was there reason to poorly pack an order and risk damage because the sales force had miscalculated shipping time. It was better to inform the customer of the mistake as opposed to delivering poorly packed merchandise. This required each team to understand the other team's role and problems. The teams learned to pick up the phone or visit with each other to discuss problems. They learned to listen to each other.

This was how synergy was developed at Fashion Plus Accessories.

Gregg felt very gratified by the results accomplished. The first year ran smoothly due to his management abilities and relationships with his associates. Camaraderie grew with every birthday celebration or group social function. Associates learned to trust Gregg, and his open door policy was greatly appreciated. Bonuses were given and the business's financial status was revealed to show that he was doing his best to grow the company, which would be good for all. With the business growth Gregg followed through with his promises to improve earnings and expand responsibilities.

14

Keeping It Under Control

VICTOR WAS ASTONISHED BY HIS FIRST BILL FROM HIS ACCOUNTANT. IT CAME with a nice looking financial statement of his first three months of operation and all the particulars, but the bill was $1,800. In a call to the accountant to have it explained, he was told that this bill was a bit higher than should be expected in the future as it included new account setup charges of approximately $500. That was little assurance to Victor as he had just barely enough money to pay his other bills for his new photography store and studio. Multiplying the expected annual total out would still be $5,000 per year, double what he had projected, and that did not include preparing the annual tax returns. After taking a deep breath to settle down, Victor decided he would have to do his own financial work. Although he had not liked the accounting course he had taken in college and did poorly, he thought maybe he should keep his own records and use his accountant strictly for tax preparation. He would discipline himself to learn how to do it. After all, it was his business and his responsibility to stay on top of the financial dealings and transactions. By posting the information himself he would know on the spot what his financial situation was. He knew of too many business owners who would have to call their accountant to find out how much money they had available or how sales compared to last year. He was determined not to be one of them and be overly dependent on an accountant.

Setting Up a System

Victor first became familiar with what records he would need to keep. The list was lengthy.

- Daily, weekly, and monthly sales journals
- Accounts payable
- Accounts receivable
- Disbursement journal
- Cash flow statement
- Payroll records
- Sales tax receipts
- Capital purchase ledger
- Inventory ledger
- Notes payable

It seemed like a lot of bookkeeping which would take hours of his time. While thirty years ago this might have been true, it is no longer. Victor found a rather simple-to-use accounting software program that would allow him to post financial information to all necessary accounts in a matter of minutes if entered on a daily basis. In addition the software would automatically compute monthly, quarterly, and annual cumulative financial statements with just a touch of a button. He also found another software program that would allow him to keep on top of exactly what his inventory level was at any time, including a notification system that alerted him to when it was time to order particular merchandise or supplies.

It took some time to learn the software applications, but the $1,800 accounting bills became a thing of the past.

The procedure. Each day Victor would post the sales from the following day and enter any checks written. The sales and services would be coded as to which category they were classified and the sales tax collected would be posted to the sales tax category. If any money due him from credit customers was received and deposited it would automatically be subtracted from the accounts receivable list. The checks written were coded as to the type of operating expense they represented. When bills were paid they would automatically be deducted from the accounts payable list, and any bank notes paid would be deducted from the notes payable journal. If any machinery or equipment was purchased, it was posted to the capital goods account. Since the totals of both sales and expenses were automatically accumulated, a working income statement was available at any time by accessing reports from the software. Victor could also pull up on a moment's notice a comparison to the last month or previous year(s) to see how they were doing.

The specific employee payroll records were kept on a separate program. This program computed pay by multiplying the number of hours worked times the hourly wage for each worker. Victor only needed to post the hours worked by each employee and any bonuses given and it would calculate the paycheck showing the amount of taxes, social security, and any other deductions. It would even print out the checks. Each employee's record was calculated and accumulated separately, providing a separate year-to-date record. The total of the paychecks would be posted to the payroll operating expense category.

The inventory system worked just as smoothly. The items sold could be transferred to the inventory control software, which would subtract the items from the inventory on hand totals. When a shipment of inventory arrived it was posted from the invoice by unit number to the inventory on hand totals. Thus there was always available a running inventory on hand list for Victor to review. A low inventory alert flashing signal served as a reminder that it was time to reorder an item. The system also made possible a quick reference to goods that were not selling well. Invoices for any goods received were posted to the accounts payable list with due date and any pertinent information regarding the shipment.

These two programs allowed Victor to be in total control of the financial aspect of his small business. He would not have to call an accountant to inquire as to the status of his business.

Forecasting and Budgeting

Budgeting is a major management planning function. The more data available, the better the forecast. As a brand-new operation Victor did not have past financial records, so initially his budget and forecast were based on his research and on industry resources. However, with every passing day the financial information accumulating in his accounting programs was easing the budget and forecasting process. He became quite expert using Excel spreadsheets as they provide a way of quickly calculating any changes in financial operations. By listing his projections in one column and then posting the results in the next it was easy to see the trends of the business operation. He would use Excel to control his budgets for sales and expenses as well as inventory on hand and on order.

At least once a week Victor would pull up the cash flow sales and expense forecast reports to enter new data and see if it was in line with expectations. In the event sales were too slow he might adjust some expenses downward, or if sales exceeded projections possibly increase his purchase plan. It also allowed him to see if expected accounts receivables were arriving on time or if there was a problem with some credit customers. He knew that if he waited too long to compare his forecast with actual numbers it would be too late to make adjustments. (See figure 14.1.)

This also allowed him to see the danger of not collecting bills on time. He was a bit too trusting in getting started and would often give wedding and special event customers thirty days to pay the remaining balance due after receiving a down payment. Many took advantage of this and the 30 turned to 60 and in some case exceeded 90 days to collect. Since Victor was paying all his expenses for extra help and equipment at the time of the event, this was causing a cash flow problem. The profits from these events, although quite good, dwindled quickly if the invoices were paid late. He found it difficult at times to pay so much out before collecting and it began showing up on the cash flow spreadsheets. He realized that if this kept up or got worse it could ruin his business even if sales and contracts were increasing. Increasing sales also meant increasing payouts before getting paid. He had heard stories of profitable businesses closing due to poor collection policies. Therefore, with the help of an attorney he drew up a simple contract

Figure 14.1

Three-month Cash Flow Spreadsheet

VIC'S PHOTOGRAPHY AND CAMERA STORE

	January	February	March
Cash on hand	$3,650	$398	$1,458
Cash receipts	3,700	6,750	5,800
Account receivable collections	600	1,600	1,200
Total cash receipts	$4,300	$8,350	$7,000
Total cash available	**$7,950**	**$8,748**	**$8,458**
Cash paid out			
Purchases	1,100	948	1,250
Wages	950	950	950
Payroll tax expense	67	67	67
Supplies	350	350	350
Advertising	450	450	450
Rent	1,050	1,050	1,050
Utilities	300	300	300
Insurance	80	80	80
Interest	165	165	165
Loan principal	300	300	300
Owner's draw	2,400	2,400	2,400
Miscellaneous	340	240	346
Total cash paid out	**$7,552**	**$7,300**	**$7,708**
Ending cash on hand	$398	$1,448	$750

that spelled out that all balances due must be paid by the conclusion of the event. All customers signed the contract, which eliminated the collection problems.

Victor also created a purchasing plan for the merchandise that was sold through his shop. His primary products were cameras, equipment, and photo albums. The vendors from whom he purchased allowed him 30 days to pay, but that was hardly enough since he placed orders for seasonal merchandise such as Christmas 90 days before the holiday. The purchase plan taught him to stagger merchandise delivery so that payments would not come due all at the same time. By forecasting his needed inventory at the first of every month he would accept delivery only on the merchandise that could reasonably be expected to sell during the thirty-day period. Therefore if he needed $4,500 of camera inventory from a certain supplier for a season he might arrange for the shipments to come in three $1,500 increments as opposed to one shipment. Although the delivery cost would be higher, it was easily offset by not suffering through cash flow problems and being forced to borrow from the bank and paying interest. If sales were running higher than forecast he would call the supplier and have them release orders sooner and possibly increase the units. If business was slow he was able to cancel or decrease the orders before being shipped and not get stuck with unwanted merchandise.

Financial Statements

The software was capable of keeping running financial statements with the push of a button. For the income statement it would show in proper format the profit or loss incurred for a particular period of time. The formula was:

REVENUES
    Less cost of goods and materials
        = Gross profit
    Less total operating expenses
        = operating profit

It was an operating profit because it did not include depreciation expense calculation on capital assets nor an accurate cost of goods cost as it did not reflect losses of inventory due to damage or theft. But it served as a gauge of comparison to objectives and could be adjusted for accuracy at the end of each fiscal year by taking a physical inventory and calculating the amount of depreciation applied to the various equipment used in the operation of the business.

Although the balance sheet was a bit more complicated, the software was able to keep an operating schedule of changes. It would adjust assets by tracking inventory totals and posting accounts receivables and adding any capital purchases to the fixed assets account. At the same time any note payments would be subtracted from borrowed debts and bill payments from accounts payable. For end-of-year accuracy depreciation of capital assets would be entered separately. The form would show as follows:

ASSETS	LIABILITIES
Current	**Current**
Cash + Accounts Payable +	
Inventory +	Current note payables
Accounts receivables =	
Total current assets	**Total current liabilities**
Fixed assets	**Long-term liabilities**
Equipment +	Bank note payable +
Leasehold improvements	Other notes payable =
Less accumulated depreciation =	
Total fixed assets	**Total long-term liabilities**
	+ Business net worth =
Total current and fixed assets	**Total liabilities and net worth**

The purpose of the balance sheet was to show the value or net worth of the business at the conclusion of a period of time. Over time as debts were paid and inventory increased, the net worth would increase. If, on the other hand, if the business needed to borrow more money the net worth would decrease. By keeping an up-to-date balance sheet Victor could easily see if his investment was growing or declining. Whenever he would meet with his bank he would take with him up-to-date financial statements prepared by his software and reviewed by his accountant.

Taxes

Victor was a sole proprietor. It was certainly the easiest way to get started as there was no formal registration except at the bank to set up a commercial account and the city to gain a business license. It also had some tax advantages, at least in the early stages of a business. As a sole proprietor he was Victor Ramsey doing business as Vic's Photography and Camera Store and he was solely responsible for all aspects of the business. This ranged from declaring all profits or losses to himself and being the legal agent for the business. He was allowed to deduct all expenses of operation including initial setup against his personal income after he declared all revenues from business activities. Since the setup costs were high his first year's profits, if any, would be low, meaning less taxes. The only tax preparation required was to attach a Schedule C form showing the income statement of the business to his standard tax form 1040. He would then post any profits or losses from the Schedule C to his 1040 and pay any taxes due. (See figure 14.2.)

The disadvantage of the sole proprietorship is that since Victor was totally responsible for all activities of the business, he was also totally liable for any harm the business might cause. If he caused an accident through reckless driving while traveling to a photo shoot or if someone was injured while in his store, Victor could be sued personally. This put at risk all his personal belongings and assets. Since he felt reasonably confident that his service was not one that would likely endanger anyone and that his personal liability insurance would be enough coverage, a sole proprietorship was the way to go, at least in the early stages.

At one time while trying to find the money to start the business he considered taking a friend as a partner. A partner would add capital and share responsibility, but Victor wanted the business to be his totally. He had heard enough stories of partnerships ruining friendships. Even if they created a partnership agreement spelling out each partner's responsibilities, how profits were to be divided, and what would happen if one partner wanted out, he was not comfortable with the arrangement. In addition, they would have to register as a partnership and declare a separate and more complex partnership tax declaration form. The additional tax reporting would be

Figure 14.2 **Schedule C Tax Form**

SCHEDULE C
(Form 1040)

Department of the Treasury
Internal Revenue Service (99)

Profit or Loss From Business
(Sole Proprietorship)

▶ **For information on Schedule C and its instructions, go to *www.irs.gov/schedulec.***
▶ **Attach to Form 1040, 1040NR, or 1041; partnerships generally must file Form 1065.**

OMB No. 1545-0074

2012
Attachment
Sequence No. **09**

Name of proprietor

Social security number (SSN)

A Principal business or profession, including product or service (see instructions)

B Enter code from instructions ▶

C Business name. If no separate business name, leave blank.

D Employer ID number (EIN), (see instr.)

E Business address (including suite or room no.) ▶

City, town or post office, state, and ZIP code

F Accounting method: (1) ☐ Cash (2) ☐ Accrual (3) ☐ Other (specify) ▶

G Did you "materially participate" in the operation of this business during 2012? If "No," see instructions for limit on losses . ☐ Yes ☐ No

H If you started or acquired this business during 2012, check here . . . . ▶ ☐

I Did you make any payments in 2012 that would require you to file Form(s) 1099? (see instructions) . . . . . . ☐ Yes ☐ No

J If "Yes," did you or will you file required Forms 1099? . . . . ☐ Yes ☐ No

Part I   Income

1	Gross receipts or sales. See instructions for line 1 and check the box if this income was reported to you on Form W-2 and the "Statutory employee" box on that form was checked . . . . ▶ ☐	1
2	Returns and allowances (see instructions)	2
3	Subtract line 2 from line 1	3
4	Cost of goods sold (from line 42)	4
5	**Gross profit.** Subtract line 4 from line 3	5
6	Other income, including federal and state gasoline or fuel tax credit or refund (see instructions)	6
7	**Gross income.** Add lines 5 and 6 . . . . ▶	7

Part II   Expenses   Enter expenses for business use of your home only on line 30.

8	Advertising	8	18	Office expense (see instructions)	18
9	Car and truck expenses (see instructions)	9	19	Pension and profit-sharing plans .	19
10	Commissions and fees .	10	20	Rent or lease (see instructions):	
11	Contract labor (see instructions)	11	a	Vehicles, machinery, and equipment	20a
12	Depletion	12	b	Other business property . . .	20b
13	Depreciation and section 179 expense deduction (not included in Part III) (see instructions). . . .	13	21	Repairs and maintenance . . .	21
			22	Supplies (not included in Part III) .	22
			23	Taxes and licenses	23
14	Employee benefit programs (other than on line 19). .	14	24	Travel, meals, and entertainment:	
			a	Travel	24a
15	Insurance (other than health)	15	b	Deductible meals and entertainment (see instructions)	24b
16	Interest:		25	Utilities	25
a	Mortgage (paid to banks, etc.)	16a	26	Wages (less employment credits) .	26
b	Other	16b	27a	Other expenses (from line 48) . .	27a
17	Legal and professional services	17	b	Reserved for future use . . .	27b

28	**Total expenses** before expenses for business use of home. Add lines 8 through 27a . . . . . . ▶	28
29	Tentative profit or (loss). Subtract line 28 from line 7	29
30	Expenses for business use of your home. Attach **Form 8829.** Do not report such expenses elsewhere . .	30
31	**Net profit or (loss).** Subtract line 30 from line 29.	
	• If a profit, enter on both **Form 1040, line 12** (or Form 1040NR, line 13) and on **Schedule SE, line 2.** (If you checked the box on line 1, see instructions). Estates and trusts, enter on **Form 1041, line 3.** • If a loss, you **must** go to line 32.	31
32	If you have a loss, check the box that describes your investment in this activity (see instructions).	
	• If you checked 32a, enter the loss on both **Form 1040, line 12,** (or Form 1040NR, line 13) and on **Schedule SE, line 2.** (If you checked the box on line 1, see the line 31 instructions). Estates and trusts, enter on **Form 1041, line 3.** • If you checked 32b, you **must** attach **Form 6198.** Your loss may be limited.	32a ☐ All investment is at risk. 32b ☐ Some investment is not at risk.

For Paperwork Reduction Act Notice, see your tax return instructions.   Cat. No. 11334P   Schedule C (Form 1040) 2012

bothersome and the liability issue did not change except that both partners would be personally liable for any action taken against them in the courts.

He recognized that eventually he might want to consider a corporate or limited liability form of ownership. Both provided limited liability, which would protect his personal assets against any legal claims. His future growth plans included working with larger clients under contractual arrangements and having a staff of 15–20 associates. Legal contracts could result in suits, and the more employees the more possibilities for negligence claims. In addition, if he grew to the expected size there would be better tax treatment options regarding insurance benefits and corporate travel and the use of corporate assets such as automobiles. Also, at that point there might be a need for raising capital, which could be accomplished by selling stock as opposed to borrowing from the bank. For now, though, it was just him and two trusted associates and the contracts for services were relatively simple. He believed he had time before making that decision. Once made there would be more reporting and regulations to follow and costs in getting the corporation started. Tax reporting complexity would increase since the corporation or a limited liability company would report taxes separately from the owners. He would be a paid executive, not an owner operator, and he would share profits with stockholders in the form of dividends. Dividends would actually be taxed twice, first as corporate profits and then as income to the recipients.

Victor also became familiar with tax preparation software. He would still use an accountant to review his taxes, but the more he did himself the less time the accountant would charge. He estimated that his handling of the bookkeeping, creating the financial statements himself, and preparing tax information in advance for the accountant saved $6,000 per year, which could be used to pay himself for the extra time devoted to taking care of the financial end of the business.

Victor was in total control of his business.

15

Your Future

SINCE YOU HAVE READ THIS ENTIRE BOOK YOU ARE VERY SERIOUS REGARDING your intentions of becoming an entrepreneur. Let's review a few final thoughts about when to start and also when to expand and when to get out.

When or When Not to Open a Business

- While there is no perfect age, the best time to become fully self-employed is when there is enough time to bounce back in the event it does not work. Starting a full-time business with a sizable investment and using your retirement savings is very risky over the age of fifty-five as you will not have time to go back to the workforce and prepare for retirement. Becoming a full-time entrepreneur under age forty provides you with the time needed to rebuild your retirement if the business does not work out by the time you reach forty-five. Young people, if able to find the finances, are in the best situation. A person in their twenties who starts a business has very little to lose as he or she probably has a minimum amount invested and has an entire lifetime to recoup their loss if not successful.

- Part-time businesses have no age limitation and are often a tremendous avenue of enjoyment and added income for semi- and retired individuals. They may also serve as an intermediary step while looking for employment after being laid off and may develop into a full-time occupation.

- Do not open a business out of desperation to find a job unless it is a secure franchise opportunity or established business. The stress will be great and the motivation may be doubtful.

- Do not open a business using your last dollar. Too many things that are out of your control can happen. Also, you will probably need to invest more money than planned during the initial three months.

- Do consider opening a business if you have a financial windfall and a great desire to succeed. Perhaps you received an inheritance, an unexpected business bonus or investment return, or maybe you hit the jackpot in Las Vegas. Many people open a business after receiving a sizable severance payment from a business which eliminated their services.

- Do accept an invitation to join a trusted colleague who can prove he has a tremendous opportunity if all he needs is your skills and abilities.

- Do consider buying a business if the opportunity represents a situation that could not be duplicated. This might come from a friend or relative who needs to move on due to retirement, illness, divorce, and so on and wants to divest without going through the hassle of putting the business on the market. Particularly if the seller is willing to finance the bulk of the selling price.

- Do consider buying a franchise that has not yet been offered to the general public but is unmistakably a good bet. Investigate closely, but those who made fortunes owning franchises were in on the very ground floor.

When to Expand

Expanding your business is exciting and ego fulfilling but also can be dangerous if not properly prepared. The desire can sometimes cloud the reality of the situation.

Proper expansion is executed by following the same research procedures as opening a new business. Collect the information regarding the market and write a new business plan.

The starting place is the profit and loss statement. You are looking for the point in time when it is necessary to expand to gain additional profits. This comes when the size of the business limits its profits due to market saturation. This is the point that profits cannot rise past a certain point without the addition of space, product line, or additional outlets. For example, if a business that has been moving forward at an acceptable pace for a number of years starts to hit a brick wall. Sales and revenues become stagnant, although there has been no change in the marketplace or additional competition. It has lost its momentum. This is called the strategic window.

The strategic window refers to that period of time when all indicators for expansion are favorable. Profits are good, competition has been weakened, the economy is strong and future demands look promising. The expansion decision is not limited to major changes. Expansion may be reached by adding a new product line or in some cases remodeling by adding additional shelving or converting storage space into selling space. If at all possible expand by making better use of the assets on hand as opposed to making a major capital outlay for a complete makeover or new location or outlet.

Just as in a new business, an expansion will take time to pay back the investment. Too many new entrepreneurs get carried away with some initial success and expand foolishly by borrowing additional monies before their business has matured. Before deciding to expand ask:

- Does the market have the necessary growth potential?
- What is the competition doing?
- Will the value added to the business produce the additional capital needed to pay back the investment in a reasonable period of time?

- Are there new markets to be served?
- Has anything happened to change the marketplace?

If you believe the answers to these questions are positive, verify and proceed. Go back to step one of the business plan. Study the demographics, do a new market analysis, a new cash flow projection, discuss with industry representatives, and make sure the expansion fits your personal and financial goals.

When to Get Out

Selling or closing a business that you have sunk your heart into may not be an easy decision. Do not let sentiment become the deciding factor. After all, you went into it with the idea of making a profit, not just to entertain yourself. You can always start another business if you have an offer that is too good to turn down. The idea is to sell high, not necessarily when you are ready. Be open to offers at any time. The key is to put the money to proper use at the time. This might mean selling out and starting another business with part of the profits, at the same time holding back enough money to reward yourself for your efforts. In addition, hopefully you had also been investing some profits into a retirement plan, just as you would deduct from a corporate salary to contribute to a 401(k) plan.

How much a business is worth will differ from industry to industry and market to market. It will boil down to what the buyer is willing to pay and your ability to convince the buyer of the value of the investment. Many theories are thrown out for arriving at a price. Some will say a year's revenues or more, other might say double or triple the value of the inventory. In reality it should be based on return of the investment to the buyer. A buyer must believe the investment will return itself in X number of years. Often five years is an acceptable rate of return as it correlates to a 20 percent return, which is more attractive than the stock market. Therefore if your business is turning a $100,000 per year profit and the future looks good you should be able to make a strong argument for a $500,000 selling price.

Don't make the mistake of holding on too long if there is a good offer. The fear of what you would do if you sold the business will be answered by your entrepreneurial mindset. Don't risk a downturn in the market or a larger competitor entering the market and damaging your business resale and costing you thousands of dollars.

One Last Thing. . .

Remember, you are not alone. There is help available so take advantage of it. Visit:

Your library. This is your greatest resource for books, periodicals, and reference materials. Don't be afraid to ask the librarian for assistance. That is why they are there and what they are trained to do. Many libraries have broadened their small business resources and some offer business seminars.

The local Chamber of Commerce. This is a good place to start your demographic search and build a local network.

Your local banker can assist you in determining what financial information is needed and where it might be found.

State and local economic agencies. These agencies are responsible for building a strong economy for the community. They want you to achieve success and should be helpful.

The closest Small Business Development Center. These offices are associated with state universities and the Small Business Administration. They offer no-charge counseling and low-cost seminars for new and existing small business owners.

Trade shows that feature suppliers to your industry. Go online and search "trade shows" for a list of shows in your area. In addition to selling products, trade shows often offer informative seminars to attendees. They are an excellent place to meet and talk to industry representatives.

SCORE offices. The Society of Retired Executives is associated with the Small Business Administration and is located near SBA regional offices. They offer free counseling from former executives in various industries.

SBA Offices. The Small Business Administration has sixteen regional offices throughout the country. They are charged with helping you, which helps the national economy.

The U.S. Department of Commerce, Office of International Trade. This is the federal agency that will assist international businesses. Check with them for upcoming trade shows and international trade agreements, monetary exchange rates, and market information that may affect your possible global business.

Best wishes for success in your entrepreneurial adventure.

BIBLIOGRAPHY

Abrams, Rhonda. *Successful Business Plans: Secrets and Strategies*. The Planning Shop, 2010.

ALA Guide to Economics and Business Reference. American Library Association, 2011.

Anderson, Max, and Peter Escher. *The MBA Oath: Setting a Higher Standard for Business Leaders*. Portfolio, 2010.

Carnegie, Dale. *How to Win Friends and Influence People*. Dale Carnegie and Associates, 1936.

Covey, Steven. *The 7 Habits of Highly Effective People*. Simon and Schuster, 1990.

Duhigg, Charles. *The Power of Habit: Why We Do What We Do in Life and Business*. Random House, 2012.

Frei, Frances, and Anne Morriss. *Uncommon Service: How to Win by Putting Customers at the Core of Your Business*. Harvard Business, 2012.

Gerber, Michael H. *The E-Myth Enterprise: How to Turn a Great Idea into a Thriving Business*. Harper, CD, 2009.

Levinson, Marc. *The Great A&P and the Struggle for Small Business in America*. Hill and Wang, 2011.

Masterson, Michael. *The Reluctant Entrepreneur*. Wiley, 2012.

Murphy, Bill. *The Intelligent Entrepreneur: How Three Harvard Business School Graduates Learned the 10 Rules of Successful Entrepreneurship*. Holt, 2010.

O'Malley, Michael. *The Wisdom of Bees: What the Hive Can Teach Business about Leadership, Efficiency, and Growth*. Portfolio, 2010.

Parsanko, Boband, and Paul Heagen. *The Leader's Climb: A Business Tale of Rising to the New Leadership Challenge*. Bibliomotion, 2012.

Ramon, Ray. *The Facebook Guide to Small Business Marketing*. Wiley, 2013.

Ramsey, Dave. *EntreLeadership: 20 Years of Practical Business Wisdom from the Trenches*. Simon and Schuster, 2011.

Riccoboni, Adam, and Daniel Callaghan. *The Art of Selling Yourself: The Simple Step-by-Step Process for Success in Business and Life*. Tarcher, 2012.

Sarillo, Nick. *A Slice of the Pie: How to Build a Big Little Business*. Penguin/Portfolio, 2012.

Schiff, Lewis. *Business Brilliant: Surprising Lessons from the Greatest Self-Made Business Icons*. Harper Business, 2013.

Stasch, Stanley F. *Creating a Successful Marketing Strategy for Your Small New Business*. Greenwood, 2010.

Taylor, Ephren W., and Rusty Fischer. *The Elite Entrepreneur: How to Master the 7 Phases of Growth & Take Your Business from Pennies to Billions*. BenBella, 2010.

Villarosa, Clara, and Alicia Villarosa. *Down to Business: The First 10 Steps to Entrepreneurship for Women*. Averty, 2009.

Weiss, Luise, Sophia Serlis-McPhillips, and others. *Small Business and the Public Library: Strategies for a Successful Partnership*. American Library Association, 2011.

Young, Lynette. *Google + for Small Business*. Que, 2013.

INDEX

Locators in **bold** refer to figures/diagrams